BENNINGTON
in
WORLD WAR II

BENNINGTON
in
WORLD WAR II

Anthony Marro

THE
History
PRESS

Published by The History Press
Charleston, SC
www.historypress.com

First published 2021

Manufactured in the United States

ISBN 9781467149228

Library of Congress Control Number: 2021941019

This history of Bennington in World War II is dedicated to my wife, Jacqueline Cleary Marro; our daughter, Alexandria Cleary Marro, who is known as "Xander"; and to all of the people of Bennington who lived through and served in the war and their children and grandchildren.

CONTENTS

INTRODUCTION

On the afternoon of December 7, 1941, Lawrence "Larry" Powers was in the living room of his family home in North Bennington, Vermont, sitting by the radio with his father and his brother Dick, listening to the Chicago Bears play the Chicago Cardinals, a game the Bears would win 34 to 24. "The announcer broke in and said the Japs had attacked Pearl Harbor," Powers recalled many years later. "We didn't even know where Pearl Harbor was."

Within a few months, more than half of those Bears would be in the service, as Powers himself would be. He was twenty-one at the time he was inducted, a graduate of North Bennington High School, where he had played basketball, and St. Joseph's Business College in Bennington, where he had earned a degree in accounting and learned how to type sixty words a minute. That last skill was important because it would keep him out of the infantry. He had gotten a job at the General Electric plant in Pittsfield, Massachusetts, thirty-nine miles away, where he rented a room during the week and generally came back home to North Bennington on the weekends. Except for a class trip to visit the 1939 New York World's Fair, where the magical new invention of television was shown to the masses for the first time, he had seldom been more than fifty miles from home. But by the time the war had ended, he had been in more than two dozen countries in Central Africa, North Africa, the Middle East and Europe, starting out as cryptographer in the Congo and ending up as a navigator on a B-24 Liberator, flying bombing raids from Italy into Austria.

Private William F. Gordon is shown in an army summer uniform, sitting on a wire fence, with a grassy field and mountains in the background. He was killed in the Battle of the Bulge. *Courtesy of the Bennington Museum.*

Bennington County is the southwestern corner of Vermont, bordered by Massachusetts to the south and by New York to the west. It had 22,286 residents in the 1940 Census, with 11,257 of them in the town of Bennington itself. Powers was one of at least 1,758 men and women from Bennington County to serve in the war, 52 of whom died and 95 of whom were wounded. Most of them were very young and seemingly had gone almost overnight from playing football for Bennington High School, hunting deer on Woodford Mountain, fishing for trout in the Battenkill River and nursing patients at Putnam Hospital to dropping bombs on Pacific Islands, parachuting from burning planes over Germany, firing M1 rifles from foxholes in Italy, nursing the sick and wounded in war zones and racing across France with Patton's tanks.

William Kearns Jr. would bayonet Japanese soldiers during a Banzai attack on Tarawa. Gedeon LaCroix would watch the raising of the flag by marines on Iwo Jima. Sergeant Donald E. White would be in the crew of the first American bomber to drop bombs on Berlin. Private William Gordon would be killed in St.Vith, Belgium, in the Battle of the Bulge, and First Lieutenant William Root II, a descendant of two Revolutionary War soldiers who had died at Bunker Hill, would be killed while trying to wrestle a revolver away from a German soldier in Beckum, Germany, just five weeks before the war in Europe ended. Captain James Fisher, the son of nationally known author Dorothy Canfield Fisher, was an army doctor who would be killed while helping rescue the survivors of the Bataan Death March from a prison camp on Luzon.

Powers, who had never been in an airplane before his flight to the Congo, ended up spending a great deal of time in them, not just during World War II, but after he was recalled to the air force during the Korean War. He retired from the air force reserves as a major in 1964. For many years, he ran the family grocery, Powers Market, in North Bennington, while also serving in the state legislature and winning several golf championships at the Mount Anthony Country Club. He lived to be ninety-three, and his funeral in February 2014 was a traditional Catholic service, with prayers, a eulogy and familiar hymns, such as "On Eagle's Wings" and "Be Not Afraid." But then, just as his son and daughter began leading the mourners out of the church, the organist suddenly cranked up the organ to full volume, and the young woman who had been singing the gentle hymns in a lilting soprano belted out in a very loud and spirited voice:

Off we go
Into the wild blue yonder
Flying high into the sun
Here they come
Zooming to meet out thunder
At 'em boys! Give 'em the gun…

Tom Brokaw, the longtime anchor of the NBC Nightly News would call the men and women of the World War II years America's "Greatest Generation." But Robert Sausville, a pilot from Bennington who flew a B-24 Liberator bomber on fifty-eight missions in the Pacific, later said that having grown up during the Great Depression, mostly without prospects for college or good paying jobs, that generation was also "a bunch of ragamuffin poor kids who didn't have anything to lose."

Sausville, who lived to be more than one hundred years old and spent his retirement years in Bennington, repairing antique clocks, was a prime example of how people could go very different ways in the war because of the simple luck of the draw. He and his Bennington High School friend Victor Racicot had enlisted the same day and trained together as aviation mechanics. They switched to pilot training on the same day and got their pilot's wings on the same day. But Sausville was then sent to the Pacific, and Racicot was sent to Louisiana. Sausville, who had married his high school sweetheart, Geraldine Marra, piloted a bomber that had shark's teeth and *Geraldine* painted on the nose. He flew fifty-eight missions and risked being shot down fifty-eight times. Racicot spent the entire war stateside, flying airmen who were training to be navigators on night flights so they could practice night navigation skills. He dropped no bombs anywhere and was never shot at.

This history of Bennington in World War II was compiled with the help of the Bennington Museum and the *Bennington Banner* newspaper, and oral histories of veterans were collected by and transcribed by the Bennington Historical Society. Two interviews were conducted by Dr. Richard Dundas and his grandson Conor Bowen. Some material also came from a play called *Bennington Goes to War* that was written by the author and

Robert LaPorte in his Marine dress uniform. His mortar unit was credited with killing seventy-five Japanese troops in a single day. *Courtesy of the LaPorte family.*

Eric Peterson, and it was staged and directed by Peterson at Bennington's Oldscastle Theatre in 2014. This book is not intended as a complete or a definitive history. The stories told here are not necessarily about the bravest or most heroic men and women who served or those who suffered the greatest. The author spent his working years as a journalist, not as a historian, and this effort is more a piece of journalism than historical record—with journalism, at best, being a first rough draft of history. But hopefully, it will give a sense of how the people of the Bennington region responded to the call to arms, both at home and abroad. And hopefully, it will be a reminder of the many sacrifices they made.

BENNINGTON

ennington was settled in 1761 by Congregational separatists from Connecticut and Massachusetts who, today, probably would be called "born again" Congregationalists. It was something of a theocracy at the start, with the original church—which was a simple frame building—also serving as the meeting house, the school and the center of government. Their leader, Captain Samuel Robinson, had passed through the area while returning from the bloody fighting at the Battle of Lake George during the French and Indian War and had decided to settle there. He and his followers bought the township that had been created by Governor Benning Wentworth of New Hampshire, who, in 1749, had begun enriching himself and his family by selling off blocks of land in what now is Vermont that were each six miles square and contained twenty-four thousand acres, the first of which he named for himself. Whether he had any right to sell them was disputed for years by New York State, which had claimed these same lands much earlier. New Hampshire's original western boundary had been, as it is today, the Connecticut River. But because both Massachusetts and Connecticut had western boundaries close to the Hudson River, Wentworth set out to match them by creating what he called the "New Hampshire Grants," which stretched west from the Connecticut River to what now is Hoosick Falls, New York. Hoosick is about fifty miles east of the Hudson, and that gave Wentworth's New Hampshire the same sort of western boundary lines that Massachusetts and Connecticut had.

New York's ongoing claim to those lands prevented Vermont from becoming the fourteenth state after the American Revolution. Instead, it became an independent republic from 1777 until 1791, during which time, it became the first place in North America to outlaw slavery. It finally became the fourteenth state after agreeing to pay New York $30,000, which was to be distributed among New Yorkers who had bought land in what later became Vermont under New York patents.

Robinson and his followers were pioneers in every sense, creating a village in what had been a wilderness with many wolves. They were also rigid in their religious beliefs, with John Spargo, the founder of the Bennington Museum, writing, "That they were men and women of narrow minds, steeped in bigotry and even fanaticism, cannot be questioned." Only Congregationalists could live in their village, which is now called Old Bennington, although they sold land to Baptists, Anglicans and others in nearby Pownal and Woodford and down in the valley that later became modern-day Bennington.

The village they created is one of the most historic in the state, and for many years, it was the de facto capital of Vermont. It was where Vermont's first newspaper was printed and where the Green Mountain Boys were organized to resist the ongoing New York claims to the land they had bought, cleared and settled. It was where Ethan Allen drank "stonewalls"—a potent mixture of hard cider and rum—night after night in Fay's Tavern and where he plotted the attack on Fort Ticonderoga during the American Revolution, saying that he had captured it "in the name of the Great Jehovah and the Continental Congress," although, in truth, he had a commission from neither. And it was the site of the large Continental army storehouse, with grain, corn, horses and cattle, that General John Burgoyne had sent close to one thousand troops to try to capture during the American Revolution in order to obtain food for his army and horses for his cavalry. Burgoyne had been marching south from Montreal to Albany in hopes of splitting New England away from the rest of the colonies, and his supply lines had become stretched thin, which made the storehouse at Bennington a tempting and important target. In addition to British troops, Tories and Natives, the force included German mercenaries who generally were known as "Hessians," although those particular troops were from the Brunswick region, not Hesse-Cassel.

What is now known as the Battle of Bennington was fought on August 16, 1777. While it is now considered a major event in Vermont history, it was actually fought in Walloomsac, New York, ten miles away from Bennington, and with troops mainly from New Hampshire and Berkshire

The Bennington Battle Monument. *Courtesy of the Bennington Museum.*

County, Massachusetts. The commander of the American troops was General John Stark of New Hampshire, who famously said at the start of the battle, "There are your enemies, the Red Coats and the Tories. They are ours, or this night, Molly Stark sleeps a widow!" Burgoyne lost 207 dead, and 700 were captured in two separate engagements during the day-long battle, while the American losses were just 30 dead and 40 wounded. That enormous loss of nearly 1,000 men from his 9,000-man army was a major cause of his defeat at Saratoga two months later. Burgoyne, who was known as "Gentleman Johnny," had warned his superiors of the threat from Vermont, writing as he moved south, "The Hampshire Grants, in particular, a country unpeopled and almost unknown in the last war, now abounds in the most active and rebellious race on the continent and hangs like a gathering storm on my left."

People from Bennington had fought in all of America's wars, and in 1941, this could be seen in the graveyard next to the magnificent Old First Church, with its Palladian windows and seating for 650 that had been modeled on the wedding cake steeples of Sir Christopher Wren's London churches and completed in 1805. The cemetery included the graves of Colonel Martin Scott, killed in the Mexican War; Colonel Newton Stone, killed in the Civil War; and about seventy-five Revolutionary War soldiers, including Captain Nathaniel Lawrence, who survived many battles only to later be kicked to death by his horse. It also had a mass grave for the British and German soldiers who had died of their wounds after the Battle of Bennington, and today, it also has the grave of David Redding, a Tory who had joined the Queen's Loyal Rangers, been captured in Bennington and hanged as a spy. He probably wasn't a spy, but he may have been a horse thief, and his trial for "inimical acts" is now seen as having been a railroading organized by Ethan Allen. "It certainly wasn't justice with a capital J," said Joseph Parks, a local historian. For many years, his bones were kept in a drawer at the Bennington Museum, but it was decided in 1976 to bury him with other British dead from the Battle of Bennington. The inscription on the tomb reads:

> *David Redding*
> *Loyalist*
> *Executed 1778*

It makes no mention of his being hanged as a spy, which is a bit like Bennington people now saying, "Sorry about that," two hundred years after the fact.

Old First Church, Old Bennington Vermont. *Courtesy of the Bennington Museum.*

By World War II, Bennington was a small city by most standards, but it was large for Vermont, where the largest city, Burlington, had about twenty-eight thousand residents, and the second-largest, Rutland, had about seventeen thousand. The original settlement had become Old Bennington, with impressive and well-maintained Georgian, Colonial Revival, Greek Revival and Federal homes, while the bulk of Bennington had moved down the hill and into the valley, where there was water to power sawmills, gristmills and, later, textile mills. At the start, the people in the valley—including many Baptists—were looked down on by the Congregationalists on the hill, who sneeringly referred to that part of town to as "Algiers." But eventually, the courthouse, post office and other government offices and all of the manufacturing plants moved down into the valley. Old Bennington became a summer colony that was inhabited mainly by wealthy people from Troy and other urban centers. It had the historic Walloomsac Inn across the street from the Old First Church and a general store next door to it, but it had no other commercial businesses at all.

Because of its location in the southwest corner of the state, Bennington was closer to the capitals of New York (Albany), Connecticut (Hartford) and New Hampshire (Concord) than it was to the Vermont capital in Montpelier. It was the home of the Bennington Battle Monument, the tallest structure in the state, and was known nationally for its pottery and stoneware, which was first produced in 1785 by a company founded by Captain John Norton, a Revolutionary War veteran. It had provided the state with five governors, including the sitting governor in 1941, William Wills, and was home to Bennington College, where Betty Bloomer (later, First Lady Betty Ford) had danced on the lawn with Martha Graham. There were five covered bridges in the area, but none were located in downtown Bennington itself.

With approximately 11,200 residents, Bennington had an Opera House, a YMCA, two movie theaters, the large and elegant Putnam Hotel, a nine-hole golf course, a U.S. National Guard Armory and a busy train station of Richardson Romanesque design. It also had Catholic, Episcopal, Methodist, Congregational and Baptist churches and many large mills. It had a strong industrial core that was surrounded by dairy farms; one of them was very large, but most of them were quite small and had fewer than twenty cows. The massive and ornate post office was made of marble, as was the train station, but most of the other prominent buildings in the village, including the old courthouse, the opera house, most of the mills and the Putnam Hotel, were made of brick. And like most New England villages, it had streets that were named for presidents and trees: Washington, Jefferson, Lincoln, Coolidge and McKinley; Beech, Hickory, Pine, Willow and Elm.

For a time in the mid-nineteenth century, it had been one of the wealthiest towns in Vermont, with the wealth coming from the mills powered by the Walloomsac River that produced many kinds of textiles. Children whose schools bordered the Walloomsac River would often rush out during recess to see what color the river was, because it often turned red, blue, yellow or green, depending on what dyes the upstream mills were using. The largest of the mills, the Leonard Holden Mill, had, at one time, employed more than eight hundred workers. And even in the 1930s, the Bradford Mill ran three separate shifts. The mills produced underwear, women's shawls, cotton and wool fabric and sewing needles, among other things, and needed so many workers that French Canadians from Quebec were recruited to staff them. The heyday of the mills came in the mid- to late nineteenth century, however, and by World War II, the textile industry had begun moving south, and much of that nineteenth-century wealth had gone with it.

Like much of Vermont, Bennington was Whiter than Sweden. Its population was mostly made up of English and Scots-Irish individuals, with the main ethnic groups being Irish and French Canadian, and it had a small but influential number of Greek and Lebanese families that ran many of the corner grocery stores and several popular restaurants. The Irish and French Canadians pretty much stayed apart from one another, with separate

Catholic parishes (Sacred Heart was the French Canadian parish, and St. Francis de Sales was the Irish parish) and separate elementary schools. The classes at Sacred Heart were taught in French by French Canadian nuns, and the children who went there never spoke English in the classroom until they got to Bennington High School.

Bennington, on the eve of World War II, had been shaped, in large part, by its summer residents, who were well-known nationally, but whose main homes and businesses were often elsewhere, and whose wealth, in several cases, had come from the California gold rush. They included the Colgate family (the creators of Colgate-Palmolive toothpaste and the benefactors of Colgate University); the Jeromes (who married into the Colgate family and, because Jennie Jerome had married Lord Randolph Churchill, were cousins of Winston Churchill); as well as the Putnam, Everett, Hall, Park and McCullough families.

Henry Putnam had been born in 1825 in the hamlet of Boquet, New York, which was just opposite of Charlotte, Vermont, on the western shore of Lake Champlain. Sometime in the 1840s, he had sailed to San Francisco, a journey that required him to cross the Isthmus of Panama by foot or by mule. He made a great deal of money, not by panning for gold, but by manufacturing a glass jar with a cork stopper that he sold to miners to keep clean drinking water in. Eventually, he developed the so-called lightning jar, which was a jar with a glass lid that was secured by a wire bale. This could be used for canning and preserving fruits and vegetables and, thus, was a forerunner of today's Mason jars. He had come to Bennington during the Civil War because his second wife's twin sister was married to Charles Dewey, a member of one of Bennington's founding families.

Portrait of Henry W. Putnam Sr. at the age of eighty-four. *Courtesy of the Bennington Museum.*

In Bennington, Putnam became the single largest landowner and manufactured canning jars, mop wringers, barbed wire, the first practical clothes wringer and other hardware items that were marketed nationally from his headquarters in New York City, where he also lived and was president of the Brooklyn Elevated Railway. He created Bennington's local hospital and water system, both of which he eventually donated to the village, and he financed one of the several volunteer fire departments, the H.W.

Putnam Hose Company. And he also created the large and elegant Putnam Hotel, which he insisted would always be a temperance hotel, with no liquor sold. That was a situation that happily changed after he died.

Edward Everett was born in Cleveland, Ohio, in 1851. He ended up in Bennington because his father died when he was three, and his widowed mother then married Henry Putnam. He went back to Ohio as an adult and invested in the glass bottling business, and by 1898, his company was producing between thirty and forty tons of glass bottles every day. More wealth came when one of his workers in Ohio struck natural gas on his property in 1887. By 1906, he owned fifty wells and was drilling four hundred others, and despite having a teetotaler for a stepfather, he was a major shareholder in the Anheuser-Busch Company, the makers of Budweiser beer, which sold much of its beer in his bottles.

In 1911, at the age of sixty, Everett decided to retire from active involvement in his businesses and commissioned George Oakley Totten to design and build a city house in Washington, D.C., that later became the Turkish Embassy and a twenty-four-room country "cottage" in Bennington

Edward Everette on horseback. *Courtesy of the Bennington Museum.*

that was modeled after a fourteenth-century Norman castle, although its red roof tiles came from Italy and were generally not found in Normandy or anywhere else in northern Europe. The exterior of the cottage was completed in a remarkably short time, just eight months, by thirty-two stone masons who Everett had brought over from Italy. Thirty-one of the masons went back to Italy, but one family—the Del Tattos—remained in Bennington and a son, Sergeant Charles Del Tatto, served in World War II and was part of the U.S. Army Air Corps unit that filmed the dropping of the atom bomb on Hiroshima. Everett called his Vermont home "The Orchards," and, in fact, it had seventy thousand fruit trees—most of them apple, but also some pear, plum, quince and cherry trees—surrounding his home on the eastern slope of Mount Anthony. His home later became Southern Vermont College, and another of his lasting impacts on Bennington was his underwriting much of the cost of transforming the old stone St. Francis de Sales Church into the Bennington Museum.

The Colgates came to Bennington in 1890, after James Colby Colgate, a New York City financier, married Hope Hubbell Conkling of Bennington, whose great-grandfather Aaron Hubbell had fought in the Battle of Bennington and whose family still lived on the Hubbell farm. Colgate used his great wealth to build a magnificent sixty-five-room mansion at the foot of Mount Anthony that he called "Ben Venue" that also had a stable for twenty horses. In 1892, he acquired the four-hundred-acre Hubbell Farm and purchased fifteen more farms to create Fillmore Farms, which eventually had about three thousand acres and employed about fifty people. At the start, the farm raised Dorset horn sheep, which came from England.

In 1912, Colgate sent his farm manager, Charles Cresson Jones, to Dorset, England, to buy more sheep from a farmer named James Foot. Jones also hired a housekeeper, Elizabeth Mellinger, to return to Bennington with him, along with her teenage daughter. The sheep made it safely to Vermont, but the Colgates had booked passage for Jones and the women on the *Titanic*. After the ship hit the iceberg on April 15, 1912, the women were put into lifeboats and survived, but Jones went down with the ship. His body was one of the very few to be recovered from the sinking of the *Titanic*, and he's now buried in the Old First Church Cemetery. Eventually, the farm switched from sheep to Ayrshire dairy cows and went into the poultry business, supplying eggs for the local market. It also had a sugar house and made a great deal of maple syrup from the trees on Mount Anthony.

The Jeromes arrived in Bennington after one of the four Colgate daughters, Hope, married William Travers Jerome Jr., a prominent

New York City lawyer. Jerome was the son of William Travers Jerome, a crusading New York district attorney who attacked racketeering before the term *racketeer* had even come into use, and he also attacked the corruption of the Democratic politicians of Tammany Hall. Jerome had also prosecuted Harry Thaw, the mentally unstable heir to a huge coal and railroad fortune, after he shot the famous architect Stanford White in 1906 at Madison Square Garden during a performance of the musical *Mam'zelle Champagne*. Thaw was obsessed about the fact that—years before he had ever met her—White had had an affair with Thaw's wife, Evelyn Nesbit, who had been the original "Gibson Girl." After a hung jury in the first trial, Thaw was acquitted in a second on the then-novel grounds of "temporary insanity." He spent several years in a mental institution but was eventually freed.

Jerome Jr. went on to become a lawyer himself, although he was not as prominent a lawyer as his father, setting up a successful law practice in Bennington after he and his wife moved there permanently in the 1930s. After he died in 1952, his widow married John Sloane, whose family owned the W. & J. Sloane furniture business. One of Sloane's daughters from his first marriage became the wife of Cyrus Vance, who was President Jimmy Carter's secretary of state. Two of Jerome Jr.'s sons served in World War II: William Travers Jerome III, who served as an officer in military intelligence in Washington, D.C., and saw no combat, and James Colgate "J.C." Jerome, who saw a great deal of combat as a sergeant with the Tenth Mountain Division in Italy, where he took part in a bayonet charge up Monte Belvedere in the Apennine Mountains and won a Bronze Star. The Tenth Mountain Division included some of the best skiers in the world and had trained in Colorado in often-brutal near-blizzard conditions. The division did little actual skiing once it got to Italy, but it did a good deal of fighting in the mountains and suffered 4,072 casualties. After he came home from the war, J.C. Jerome finished college at Cornell, became the president of Fillmore Farms and also took control of the Mount Anthony Country Club in Bennington, where, as an excellent golfer, he won several Vermont Amateur State Championships.

J.C. Jerome's great-grandfather Lawrence Jerome was a brother of the Leonard Jerome who was the father of Jeanette "Jennie" Jerome. Jennie had married Lord Randolph Churchill and was the mother of Winston Churchill, making J.C. Jerome a cousin of the British prime minister. J.C. was the only one of Churchill's American relatives to see combat, fighting Germans in the Apennine Mountains while Churchill was meeting with Stalin and Roosevelt in Yalta to discuss the postwar reorganization of Germany and Europe.

This photograph of Governor Hiland Hall and his wife, Dolly Tuttle David Hall, is listed as P 1966.1994.6. *Courtesy of the Bennington Museum.*

Also contributing greatly to Bennington as it existed at the time of the attack on Pearl Harbor were the Hall, Park and McCullough families of North Bennington. Hiland Hall, the son of one of the original settlers in Bennington, was born in Bennington in 1795. He was a governor of Vermont and a congressman who also was a historian and the leading organizer of the building of the battle monument. He insisted on calling the fight against Burgoyne the "Battle of Bennington," even though the British and Germans had always called it the "Battle of the Walloomsac." But once the battle monument was built, it became the Battle of Bennington, and the battle site is now known as the Bennington Battlefield, even though it's located entirely in Rensselaer County, New York.

In 1851, Hall was named chairman of the U.S. Land Commission that was created to settle the land title disputes in California that resulted from claims by Americans to what had been Mexican-owned land before Mexico had to give up California after its defeat in the Mexican-American War. He relocated to San Francisco to do this, and his son-in-law Trenor Park went with him.

Park had been born in 1823 in Woodford, where his father, Luther, was a logger and surveyor. He had been named for Thomas Trenor, the Irish shipbuilder who had helped organize the failed rebellion against the British in 1798 and had been the only organizer to escape hanging, which he may have done by disguising himself as a dead man and escaping in a coffin. Trenor had ended up in Bennington, where he purchased a blast furnace in Furnace Grove and became friends with Park's father.

Park married Hall's daughter Laura in 1846. He was a small and slender man, and vintage photographs show him head to head with Laura and much slimmer. He was the proprietor of a candy store on Bennington's Main Street when he was just fifteen, and later, he read law in the office of Bennington County's state attorney. It was likely a conflict of interest for him to represent clients who were seeking land rulings from his father-in-law, but he did it and made considerable money doing it. His real wealth, however, came from managing the hugely rich Rancho Las Mariposa Gold Mine that was owned by John C. Fremont, the explorer, politician and military man who had taken control of California during the Mexican-American War and who would later represent the state in the U.S. Senate.

In 1864, Park returned to Vermont, where he created the First National Bank of North Bennington, invested in the Central Vermont Railroad and purchased a controlling interest in the Panama Railway. He was elected to the state legislature and served as a trustee of the University of Vermont. Although he was maintaining a large house in Manhattan, he bought two hundred acres of land from his father-in-law in 1864 and built a thirty-five-room Second Empire–style mansion that became his family's summer home. His eldest daughter, Eliza Hall Park, known as "Lizzy," married John G. McCullough, who Trenor Park had known in California and who eventually managed many of Park's holdings for him. When McCullough ran for governor of Vermont in 1902, his backers often referred to him as "General McCullough." Many of the Vermont governors in the preceding four

Left: Portrait of Trenor Park. *Produced by the Metropolitan Publishing & Engraving Company of Boston, courtesy of the Bennington Museum.*

Right: Head-and-shoulders portrait of John G. McCullough, the governor of Vermont from 1902 to 1904. *Courtesy of the Bennington Museum.*

decades had been Civil War veterans, and calling McCullough "General" was likely intended to suggest Civil War service. However, the title, in fact, came from his having been the attorney general of California at an early age—he had never served in the Civil War.

Hall had been the main backer of the Bennington Battle Monument. Park, along with Seth Hunt, had given Bennington its library and veterans' home, and he had created both the National Bank in North Bennington and the handsome Victorian train station there. The McCulloughs had given North Bennington its library and fire department and had been largely responsible for the creation of Bennington College. One of their daughters, Laura Jennings, had given her home to the college for use as a music building, and Jennings Hall would later serve as the model for the home in Shirley Jackson's gothic horror novel *The Haunting of Hill House*.

So, by the time the war began, these families, between them, had largely been responsible for the area's battle monument, hospital, water system, two libraries, two volunteer fire companies, opera house and most fashionable hotel, along with the Mount Anthony Country Club, the Bennington Museum, Bennington College and the Vermont Veterans' Home. They also created the Everett Orchards and the huge Fillmore Farm, both of which employed many workers.

In addition to the previously mentioned organizations, Bennington, in 1941, also had a minor league baseball team, the Bennington Generals. For one summer, in 1940, the first baseman was the tall and lanky Kevin Joseph Aloysius Connors, who was a student at Seton Hall. Connors eventually played professional baseball for the Chicago Cubs and professional basketball for the Boston Celtics, which he didn't play particularly well. After he became famous as Chuck Connors of the wildly popular television show *The Rifleman*, one of his former teammates from the Celtics said that he had gone from being "the worst shot in the east to the best shot in the west."

The United States Army, in 1940, had only 190,000 regular troops, which made it the seventeenth largest army in the world, even smaller than the army of Romania. But once Germany attacked Poland in 1939, concerns grew that the army needed to expand quickly, and President Franklin Roosevelt ordered the mobilization of the national guard for serious training. As part of this, the Bennington Company of the Vermont National Guard, Company I, was mobilized in February 1941 as part of the Forty-Third Infantry Division, which would eventually become known as the "Winged Victory Division" because its commander in the South Pacific was General Leonard F. "Red" Wing of Rutland.

One of the young men in the company was Joseph Krawcyz, whose parents had been born in Poland. Krawcyz was nineteen, having just graduated from Bennington High School. "I could see the war coming," he said in an interview conducted by Anne Bugbee of the Bennington Historical Society in 2000. "I figured if I joined the guard and if we did go to war, I'd go with people I knew. That's the main reason I joined the guard instead of waiting to be drafted. I joined to be with Bennington boys."

Krawcyz's company trained first at Camp Blanding, Florida, and then at Camp Shelby, Mississippi. The pay was thirty dollars a month for a private—a dollar a day—that was later increased to fifty dollars a month. So, by the time Pearl Harbor was bombed, Bennington already had an infantry company mobilized, although it contained fewer than 100 of the more than 1,700 men and women from Bennington County who eventually served in the war. Krawcyz himself would get a battlefield commission, survive machine gun and shrapnel wounds and be awarded a Silver Star for gallantry in action at Ipo Dam in the Philippines, where the Forty-Third Division incurred casualties—120 dead and 515 wounded—while killing more than 2,700 Japanese and capturing 115 more.

THREE MARINES

Early in 1942, Leonard Morrison, a balding and portly middle-aged attorney who was very much 4-F and thus excluded from the service, drove two Bennington friends down to Pittsfield, Massachusetts, to enlist in the U.S. Marine Corps. The pair were William F. Kearns, known as "Billy," and Gedeon LaCroix, known as "Onion." LaCroix had been a freshman at the University of Vermont on Pearl Harbor Day, and Kearns had been a freshman at St. Lawrence University in Canton, New York.

LaCroix had played football, basketball and baseball in high school and had also played trumpet in the school band. Kearns had been the sports editor of the high school newspaper and also covered high school sports for the *Bennington Banner*. He had so angered the football coach with his early coverage that the coach refused to let him ride the team bus to away games. The Kearns family didn't have a car, but Morrison was a family friend who went to most of the football games, and Kearns called him from the payphone at the YMCA and asked if he could ride with him to the first out-of-town game that he couldn't ride the team bus to. Morrison told him to wait outside the YMCA, and a short time later, a car pulled up to the curb with Morrison's brother at the wheel and Morrison in the passenger seat. He motioned Kearns into the car, telling him as he slid into the back seat, "We didn't think we should leave the adjectives at home."

It was Morrison who later persuaded Kearns to attend college and who drove him to St. Lawrence to tour the campus and fill out the application forms for admission and financial aid. So, it was Morrison who, in ways that

Pictures of Bill Kearns and Gedeon LaCroix in marine dress uniforms. *Courtesy of the Bennington Museum.*

we'll discuss later, was responsible for much of what we now know about Bennington during World War II, who drove Kearns first off to college and then off to war.

LaCroix had to get his parents' approval to enlist because he hadn't yet turned eighteen. His father, who had been in the artillery in World War I, told him that the marines had taken the brunt of the action in that war and that he should join any branch of the service except the marines. But he and Kearns were inducted in Pittsfield, took the train from Springfield, Massachusetts, to Parris Island, South Carolina, and went through boot camp together; LaCroix later said that they wondered if they'd made the right choice because the training there was so rough and demanding.

From there, they went to advanced training at Camp LeJeune, North Carolina; its fourteen miles of oceanfront beach made it well-suited for practicing the sort of amphibious assaults that the marines specialized in. And from there, they went together to Camp Eliot, near San Diego, and then were shipped out to Aukland, New Zealand, on a banana boat that had been converted into a troop carrier. The ship was the *Moore & McCormack*, "Mormacport," which took a month to get from California to New Zealand. "Everybody was sick," LaCroix recalled many years later. "The first night out, I was so sick that I threw up all night long. The ship was a hellhole because the bunks were stacked 12 high in the holds. It was so hot down there that everybody was trying to sleep on the deck. I later discovered that a good friend of mine that I was in high school with was onboard the ship and was in the same 1st Battalion that I was. That was Robert LaPorte, who was another French boy who went to the [same] French grammar school in Bennington that I did."

LaCroix and LaPorte would serve in the same battalion throughout the war, but once they landed in Aukland, Kearns went in a different direction. LaCroix and LaPort would serve with the Twenty-First Regiment of the Third Marine Division. Kearns would serve with the Sixth Regiment of the Second Marine Division, which was known as the "Pogey Bait Marines." That nickname came from the fact that marines in China, before World War II, were issued candy bars like Baby Ruths and Tootsie Rolls as part of their rations. This was a time when sugar and other assorted sweets were rare in China and in high demand by the Chinese. And the ship that took the Sixth Marines to Shanghai in 1931 had been loaded so hurriedly and so haphazardly that the ship's store ended up with ten thousand candy bars but only two bars of soap. Once in Shanghai, the candy was used to barter, particularly with prostitutes. The Chinese word for prostitute, roughly translated, was *pogey*, so the candy bars thus became "pogey bait," and the Sixth Marines, with their huge supply of candy bars, became the "Pogey Bait Marines."

Kearns would survive a Banzai attack on Tarawa and would be wounded on Saipan. For many years after the war, at a time when he was one of the most important officials in Vermont's state government, Kearns would have nightmares about bayonetting Japanese soldiers in hand-to-hand combat. He was promoted first to corporal and then to sergeant and eventually received a Bronze Star for bravery and a Purple Heart. The award was for refusing to leave his radio after being wounded on Saipan. In describing the awards ceremony in a letter to his parents, he wrote, "There was the usual parade, band, formation, and the general presenting the awards." And then, taking note of the popular 1941 movie *Sergeant York*, in which Gary Cooper plays America's World War I hero Sergeant Alvin York, who, on October 18, 1918, singlehandedly had killed 25 Germans and captured 132 others

Picture of Robert LaPorte with his mother at their home on Dewey Street in Bennington. *Courtesy of the LaPorte family.*

during the Argonne offensive and who was later kissed on both cheeks by the French general as he pinned a Croix de Guerre medal on him, Kearns added, "I felt like Sgt. York, only I didn't get the French kiss."

LaPorte was the fourth child in a family of eight. He had six sisters and one brother, and at the time of the Pearl Harbor attack, he was working as a machinist in the Colt Firearms Plant in Hartford, Connecticut. In September 1942, one of his friends there was drafted, and LaPorte, his friend and three others went to New York City for a weekend of partying before the friend left for the service. At the last minute, the friend decided that he wanted to enlist instead of being drafted, and the other four decided to join him and enlisted on the spot. LaPorte and one other went into the marines, a third went into the army and the other two enlisted in the navy.

Each of the companies in the Twelfth Marine Regiment of the Third Marine Division had two hundred men, and LaPorte's company had a rifle squad, a mortar squad and a machine gun squad. He was in the mortar squad, which had a sixty-millimeter mortar. The squad leader would carry the sights for the mortar; the gunner would carry the mortar tube; and a third man would carry the tripod. Three other men with each six-man mortar unit would carry ammunition. LaPorte's unit went from New Zealand to American Samoa for supplies and then to Guadalcanal for mopping up operations and more training before moving on to Bougainville in the Solomon Islands.

"As far as I'm concerned, this was one of the worst experiences I've ever had—just the living conditions on Bougainville," he later said.

When you're in the jungle, you don't see the sun—only when it's high noon. You go down and look at the people that are on the beach, and they've got a beautiful tan. But we were pale white because we never saw the sun. The insects were terrible, plus the living conditions were so bad that a lot of the boys developed what the natives called "MuMu," which was elephantiasis. It was a deterioration of the joints, like the knees, and the testicles could have a lot of swelling. The ones that had it real bad would be sent to a cold climate like Canada to recover. We also had jungle rot that formed blisters, especially on your feet and ankles, and those blisters would bleed and make more blisters. Some of the boys had to have amputations because the rot got into their bones.

It was on Bougainville that LaPorte became involved in serious fighting in jungle growth that was so dense he couldn't see three feet in front him. "As a rule, a mortar squad is behind the riflemen," he said.

The riflemen make the front line. The mortar squad is behind them and fires the mortars over their heads into the enemy. Well, the enemy was so close to us that I couldn't use the tripod and couldn't use the sights. I had to take the barrel of the mortar out of the tripod and put it in my helmet and fire it almost straight up, which is against the rules because it could come back down on you or on the boys who are directly in front. But we had to take that risk because the Japs were really on us. They were right in our faces. We fired and fired and fired. We killed quite a few Japs, and we didn't lose a man.

The *Bennington Banner* later printed a story saying that the marines had issued a press release saying that LaPorte and his mortar crew had killed at least seventy-five Japanese troops that day.

Eventually, LaPorte ended up on Iwo Jima, where he and LaCroix watched the flag raising there. That was also where he was wounded and removed from combat.

The men in combat—they're all buddies. They were closer to me than my brother and sisters. We lived together twenty-four hours a day. We ate, slept, played, fought and did everything together. And when one of them got hurt or got shot, it just demoralized you. I remember one buddy of mine who was in the foxhole—well, it wasn't a foxhole because we didn't have foxholes on Iwo Jima. The soil was nothing but ash, and when you started making a hole, it would just start caving in, so all you had was an indention in the ground. We were just sitting there, waiting for action to resume, and all of a sudden, he just keeled right over. He got shot right between the eyes and fell right into my lap.

Later, he continued:

I don't think I had any fear at all. We were trained so good that everything went like clockwork. This is one thing I always admired about the marine corps. I don't know what it is like today, but our training back then was excellent. We knew when we hit the beach what we were supposed to do and when to do it, and we did it as best we could.…

I was only on Iwo Jima ten days before I was wounded by a hand grenade. That was late in February 1945. It was at night, and we always had two in the hole, and of course, it wasn't much of a hole. It was just a dent in the ground. I was with Sergeant Tippany, and I was on watch, and I could see some sparks from below coming towards me. I jumped on top of Tippany and I said, "Cover up. I think a grenade is coming." And I'd just got that out of my mouth when the grenade exploded, and I was right on top of him. He didn't get touched at all, and I got hit with shrapnel. I got hit in the hand and the wrist and in the leg and ribs. That put me out of commission. I was evacuated from Iwo Jima to Guam by boat and then was flown to Hawaii. I was first in the hospital and when released from the hospital, I was put on guard duty at the base. That's where I was on V-J Day.

A few months after he returned to the United States, he received a citation dated August 18, 1945, signed by Major General G.B. Erskine, the commander of the Third Marine Division. It read: "For meritorious service in action against the Japanese while serving as squad leader. His aggressive and courageous action throughout these campaigns was a constant inspiration to the men of his platoon. His skill and courageous devotion to duty were in keeping with the highest traditions of the U.S. Naval Service."

LaCroix, meanwhile, was still on Iwo Jima. Like LaPorte, he had served on Guadalcanal, which had pretty much been secured by the time the Third Marine Division landed there. And like LaPorte, he saw his first fighting on Bougainville, where he was a scout, going on patrols through the jungle ahead of the main body. "That wasn't much fun," he recalled in his interview with the Bennington Historical Society more than fifty years later. "It's very frightening when you get about twenty yards in the jungle, and you can't see anyone behind you, and all of a sudden, you find a dead marine right in front of you, and you wonder how he got there."

As the marines worked their way from one island to another, LaCroix landed on Guam, which involved six weeks of fighting. "The Japanese were much better soldiers than we were because they were so thoroughly indoctrinated, both religiously and to the emperor, that they would rather die than be captured," he said.

We preferred to stay alive. It was largely through our supremacy in firepower that we were able to defeat the Japanese. We were engaged with soldiers who were fanatics. They broke through our lines, almost drove us back to the beach with their Banzai charges. In one case where they broke through our lines, they were all drunk. They had a lot of whiskey and saki. They fortified themselves with liquid confidence. There was a lot of hand-to-hand combat in those charges. They killed a lot of people. When daylight broke, we had to find snipers who hadn't been killed. I remember one sniper who had killed about five marines. We finally found out where he was holed up. Then we heard the hand grenade. He just took his hand grenade and held it to his stomach and blew himself to bits. They were very, very determined to defend themselves and to die for the emperor.

Guam was bad, but Iowa Jima was worse. It was bombed seventy-two days in a row before the marines landed, and battleships pounded it with sixteen-inch shells. But the Japanese had their heavy artillery in caves, and when the marines landed, they pulled out their big guns and wreaked havoc on the beaches. The marines had to take Mount Suribachi first, because that's where the Japanese had their communications center for the entire island. "I was in a foxhole when I saw the very famous flag raising, which is now the *Iwo Jima Memorial*. I saw the flag go up. I said to my buddy, Bob LaPorte, who was in the foxhole with me, 'Well, there goes Old Glory. They'll report it back in the states, and everyone will think the island has been secured.'

Gedeon LaCroix in combat fatigues on Iwo Jima. He has a bandage on his right hand. *Courtesy of the Bennington Museum.*

But we hadn't even started fighting." In fact, the fighting lasted for thirty-one more days, and of the 22,060 Japanese on the island, 21,844 were killed or committed suicide. Only 216 were taken prisoner. There were 26,000 American casualties, including 6,800 deaths. It was the only time during the war that the American casualties in a battle exceeded those of the Japanese, and there was much criticism and second-guessing afterward about whether the Americans should have fought there at all. One retired admiral was quoted in *Newsweek* as saying it wasn't worth the number of casualties to capture what he called "a small God-forsaken island useless to the army as a staging base and useless to the navy as a fleet base." But it was later revealed that Iwo Jima was considered a crucial emergency landing point for the B-29s that carried the atom bombs that were dropped on Japan.

LaPorte and LaCroix were wounded there. LaPorte was removed from combat, but LaCroix was just bandaged up and sent back into action. Lawrence Gates of Bennington was killed there. "Almost everybody got hit with something there," LaCroix said.

> *I got shrapnel wounds. My intelligence unit was totally decimated. I ended up becoming in charge of the battalion intelligence unit and got promoted from pvt. 1st class to corporal....I also captured the first Japanese on Iwo Jima. We had to learn Japanese phrases. I was just poking through some caves and shouted into one. This little emaciated old Jap, starving and wounded, came out of the cave. I was afraid others were going to want to shoot him, but I got him back to battalion headquarters safely, so he survived.*

LaCroix was still on Iwo Jima when the war ended, working on maps and plotting the landing of his unit in Japan. Then suddenly, one night, at 10:00 or 11:00 p.m., he suddenly heard the headquarters band playing and found everyone shouting and screaming that the war was over. And he had enough active duty points under the points system that he could be among the first to leave for the United States. His colonel told him that, having fought all the way from the Solomon Islands, he should stay and take part in the occupation of Japan. "No thanks, Colonel. I have no desire," LaCroix told him. "There's only one place I want to go, and that's home."

***

LAPORTE CAME BACK TO Bennington and owned and operated Bennington Tile before buying and managing the local bus station. He and his wife had four children. When he died at the age of eighty-five in 2007, his obituary in the *Bennington Banner* said, "He found joy in the simple things of life: fishing early in the morning, tending to his vegetable garden, picking apples that his son grew, dancing and watching the sunset with his wife. Bob made a mean apple pie."

LaCroix went to Middlebury College on the GI Bill and then got an MBA from Wayne University. He spent thirty-five years in the steel industry, mostly in Pittsburgh, ending up as a vice-president, overseeing four mills and a fleet of ships. For retirement, he came back to Bennington County, where he collected antiques and for many years was a trustee of the Bennington Museum. He was still mowing his large lawn on his lawn tractor in 2020, which made him one of the last people—and maybe the very last person—who had seen the flag raising on Iwo Jima who was still alive.

Bill Kearns went to work as a reporter for the *Bennington Banner* and eventually became the state's commissioner of administration during the administration of Governor Philip Hoff, making him one of the most senior officials in Vermont government. In all, he worked for five governors. He and his wife had a son and three daughters, and he was eighty-nine years old when he died in 2011.

THE TWINS

James Albert Merrow Jr. and Joseph Arthur Merrow were identical twins who were born in Bennington on May 14, 1921, and graduated from Bennington High School in 1940. They seem to have been quiet young men. Throughout high school, they played no sports, joined no clubs and took part in no extracurricular activities. But together, they landed at Utah Beach on D-Day, took part in the Battle of the Bulge and went into Germany with Patton's tanks. Each came back home with five battle stars.

James talked about their wartime experiences in the spring of 2000 in an interview with Anne Bugbee of the Bennington Historical Society. He was working at the Benmont Paper Company as a stock clerk at the time of the attack on Pearl Harbor, he said, and he went to the army recruiting station to enlist. "I walked in, and the recruiter, a big burly guy, said, 'How can I help you?' I said, 'I want to enlist in the army.' He looked at me, and he sort of smirked. He said, 'Listen, kid. You'd better go home and grow up.' I was completely disgusted and left. It's funny the number of people I've talked to who tried to enlist, were turned down and then were drafted."

Merrow and his brother were drafted on March 17, 1942, in what was called the "father-son draft" because it was for men between the ages of eighteen and forty-five. Because it was St. Patrick's Day, the numbers were in green capsules that were drawn from a large glass bowl in Washington, D.C., by the secretary of war. The Merrows sat by the radio, listening to the draft numbers being called, and in the very first hour of what was going to be an all-night event, first Joseph's number, then James's number and then their

James Merrow's high school yearbook picture. *Courtesy of the Bennington Free Library.*

father's number were drawn. Their father had been born in 1920 and was forty-two years old at the time.

In the end, their father wasn't called, but the Merrow twins were sent to Rutland for physicals and were classified 1-A and fit for combat. On August 18, they boarded a train in North Bennington and, along with forty-five others, were taken to Fort Devens in Ayer, Massachusetts, and then sent to Fort Lee in Virginia. At Fort Lee, although they had no experience at all with engines, they were assigned to automotive repair. They then went to Holabird Motor Base near Baltimore, where they learned to repair motorcycles and then were sent by train to Pomona, California, where the camp had no motorcycles at all and, instead, had them installing spare parts to repair tanks and trucks.

Eventually, James was told he was going to be transferred to the 460th Ordnance Evacuation Company, even though he had no idea what an ordnance evacuation company was, and he was told that his brother was going to be sent to a different unit. Their mother had told them repeatedly to try to stay together and watch out for one another—to the point that James had turned down an opportunity for officer candidate school so that he could stay with Joseph. So, the pair of them went to their colonel and said they wanted to stay together, and he said that since the five Sullivan brothers in the navy had all been killed when their ship, the USS *Juneau*, was torpedoed during the Battle of Guadalcanal, the military had a policy of putting family members in different units. But he thought it over for a few minutes and told them they could stay together. So, the pair of them ended up with the ordnance evacuation company, which had tank retrievers—the largest vehicles in the army, with fourteen wheels—that were used to recover damaged tanks and bring them back for repair.

"We trained in the Mojave Desert for something like five months, mostly at night because it was so hot in the daytime," James said. Eventually, they sailed from New York to England on the HMS *Aquitania*, landing in Scotland and then being taken by train to a camp just outside Salisbury, England. They were there for several months when, suddenly, one day, they were told they were going to Portsmouth.

We were quarantined at Portsmouth—couldn't write to anyone, no communication with the outside—so we knew it was D-Day. Then, a few days later, we saw paratroopers going overhead, the planes and the gliders. It seemed as though there were hundreds of them. We stood outside in the dark and looked at them and said, "This is it." D-Day had started.

Three days later, we were ordered down to the port with our equipment. We were put on the LCT (a landing craft for tanks) and went ashore. We landed on Utah Beach, luckily, and we landed in the wrong place on Utah Beach, luckily, because…we had casualties but nothing like they had on Omaha Beach. Everything seemed to be confusion. There were so many explosions of artillery and everything you can think of. There was a landing craft right next to us that got hit. One minute, it was there, and the next minute, there was nothing—just pieces of flesh that fell down on everyone. We were stunned, but we finally landed and went forward as best we could, having a lot of casualties.

In the days after landing, the brothers helped transport tanks to the front lines and brought disabled tanks back for repairs or to take parts from damaged tanks and use them to repair other tanks. After the battle of Saint Lô, their unit was transferred from the First Army to the Third Army, which was commanded by General George Patton.

What a change! Boy, oh boy. It was extreme. We could never sit down to eat. There was sleep deprivation. You slept where you could and when you could—under trucks, in the mud, anywhere. But you had to be ready to move constantly, which we did. There was no day or night, sort of. It was always forward, keeping the enemy off balance.

General Patton used to come up and tour the area. If there was a tank that wasn't moving, he wanted to know why. Someone's head was going to roll. We really started moving after Saint Lô. We took many German prisoners. We retrieved and returned many, many tanks. But there were several horrible aspects to retrieving a tank. If a tank was hit with an incendiary shell, the screams were terrible. Sometimes, you could see through the tanks because they were so hot when the ammunition rack was hit. Then, other times, the tanks were hit with high-velocity shells that went right through them. What happened then was that the crew died of concussion because the shell going through displaced the air. They sat in their bucket seats, still at their stations. There was not a scratch on them, except a little bit of blood around the nose. Their eyes were wide open. But they were dead because of the concussion.

The brothers moved across France with Patton's army for more than four months, when suddenly, the Germans counterattacked in the Ardennes in what became known as the Battle of the Bulge.

It was an awful experience. It was cold, windy and damp in the forest. We couldn't see the Germans very often. They couldn't see us. There was a lot of wild firing. We had to dig tanks out and bring them back for repair, but the roads were crowded. They were dirt roads, and our vehicles were slipping off. When our big retriever slipped off and hit trees, they snapped right off like they were toothpicks. We did this for weeks and took a lot of prisoners, but then, we were told, "No more prisoners, especially SS."

The Waffen-SS were a military branch of the Nazi Party that fought alongside regular German Army troops and later were charged with many war crimes. But during the Battle of the Bulge, Merrow saw an American officer tell several of his men to take nine captured SS troops and execute them, which they did.

"We were fortunate that, as a unit, we survived the ordeal in the Ardennes," Merrow said.

It was very, very heavily wooded. It reminded me a lot of Vermont, but it was mostly evergreens and cedars. The Germans would set the fuse on their shells to explode in the treetops because, in addition to the regular shrapnel, there would be pieces of wood that could kill you. I got hit in the eye with a piece of wood. I couldn't see. Blood was running down my face. They examined my eye and said they didn't know whether I was going to lose it or not. But I was lucky, and I didn't.

The Merrow twins eventually went on into Germany with Patton's tanks, and James was particularly happy to see the cathedral at Cologne, which was left standing while the rest of the city was virtually destroyed. When the war in Europe ended, the twins were transferred to the Sixty-Sixth Infantry Division, the so-called Black Panther Division, and were scheduled to go to the Pacific. But the war ended just as they got back to the states, and they were discharged. They were twenty-three years old at the time and had been in the service for three and a half years.

***

JOSEPH MERROW REMAINED A bachelor and spent his life as an educator. James apparently used every dime of GI Bill money that he was entitled to in order to get several degrees. He was accepted at the University of Oklahoma and went to Norman to enroll. When his counselor learned that he was from Bennington, he said, "What the heck are you doing out here? You've got Bennington College right in your own back yard." James told him that Bennington was just for girls and was told that there always had been a few men at the school, mostly for roles in drama and dance, and that he could save a lot of housing and travel money by going there. So, Merrow enrolled at Bennington, got a bachelor's degree and then did graduate work at North Adams State College, which is now the Massachusetts College of Liberal Arts. He then was accepted at the University of Paris and the Ecole des Beaux Arts, where he wanted to study painting. That was where he met the young Paris-born Pierrette Blot, who became his wife. He returned to Bennington with his wife and her three sisters and taught for many years at the local high school.

Joseph died in 1982, and James died in 2001.

4

LARRY POWERS

O n the day after the Japanese attacked Pearl Harbor, Lawrence "Larry" Powers and several unmarried friends from the General Electric plant in Pittsfield went to the army recruiting station during their lunch break and said they wanted to enlist. They were told that they were in critical defense jobs and couldn't enlist, even though they wanted to. But a few months later, in March 1942, there was the St. Patrick's Day draft drawing, and Powers's number was the eighth one drawn from the fishbowl. He was then told that his critical job classification had been withdrawn, and he was listed as 1-A for the draft. "Here I was, twenty-one years old and green as grass and about to go off and join the army," he recalled many years later. "I had never been farther from home than a class trip to the New York World's Fair. By the time the war ended, I'd been in more than two dozen countries."

Powers was assigned to the U.S. Army Air Corps and sent by train to Miami Beach for testing and training. The group he was with was put up in a hotel, not a barracks, and he had a room about twenty-five yards from the beach. "When we got through for the day, we all headed for the ocean and had a great time swimming. One night, I pulled guard duty on the beach. We were armed with baseball bats and told to be on the alert for saboteurs that might come ashore from a German submarine just offshore."

After two weeks of testing and training, Powers was told he was eligible for four different military specialties. One of them was cryptography, for which he had to be able to type forty words a minute. That was no problem for him, because he had to type sixty words a minute to get out of business college. After he passed the typing test, he was told that if he went to cryptography training, he would be in training for six months, and after finishing, he would have to serve at least a year in the United States before being eligible for overseas duty. "Being somewhat timid, this sounded good to me, and I felt that things were a heck of a lot safer here in the good old U.S.A.," he said. He didn't even know what cryptography was, and when he asked, he was told that it had something to do with secret codes. "It's a brand-new school, and they haven't got it all worked out yet," he was told.

Sergeant Lawrence Powers of North Bennington is shown in his United States Army Air Corps uniform. He was originally a cryptographer in the Belgian Congo and then a navigator on a bomber based in Italy. *Courtesy of the Bennington Museum.*

The bottom line was that the training didn't last six months, and he didn't get to spend the following year in the United States. Right after the training ended—just ten weeks after he had been inducted—he and another cryptographer were given sealed orders and put on a C-47 aircraft, which was a transport plane most commonly used to drop paratroopers. "I had never been on an airplane before. When they closed the doors, a lieutenant opened our orders and said, 'You guys are going to the Belgian Congo.'"

Powers ended up in Elizabethville, which, back then, had a population of about fifty thousand, with the central city reserved for white people, mostly Belgians with some clusters of British, French, Italian and Greek individuals. Black people were not allowed in the central city after dark, except for house servants, who lived in shacks behind the European-style city homes. The total U.S. military force there was just six men—two radio operators; two cryptographers, who converted messages from code into plain text; a maintenance man; and a commanding officer, a Lieutenant McAllister who Powers never saw very much of. The unit was billeted in a French hotel, where they were charged $3.50 a day for rooms and meals. They made out well with that arrangement because the air corps gave them $7.00 a day in expense money.

When we moved into the hotel, we found that there was only one bathroom for the whole hotel. There were six toilets and six bidets. I waited two days before I was able to get into the bathroom alone. As I was sitting there, contemplating this strange system, a lady came in and sat down right beside me. It didn't seem to bother her, but I was a kid from North Bennington, and it sure bothered me.

Powers was transferred from the Congo to Egypt and was based in Cairo. During various leaves, he traveled to Tunisia, Morocco and the Holy Land. But eventually, he applied for flight training and was rotated back to the United States as an aviation cadet, first going to flight training in San Antonio and then navigation training at Hondo, Texas. "Whenever I hear the phrase *chicken shit* I immediately think of Hondo," he said.

We ran from formation to formation. We "yes, sired," and "no, sired," and "no excuse, sired." But the navigation training itself was very good, and in March 1945, I joined the Fifteenth Air Force in Taranto, Italy. You had to fly thirty-five missions before you could get rotated back to the states. When I first went into the tent I was to stay in, I saw three names written on the roof over the bunk assigned to me. After each name was a series of marks. I found out that each mark represented one mission. One name had sixteen marks, one name had twenty-eight marks, and one had only four marks. I didn't think I had been given a very good bunk as far as completing a tour of combat was concerned.

We flew a four-engine B-24 bomber. We didn't have a bombardier on our crew. That meant that, as navigator, I would drop all the bombs. The controls were set by bombardiers before we left the ground. All I had to do was to arm two switches, and when I saw the bombs drop out of the plane in front of me, I would toggle the switch, and our bombs would automatically drop right along with the others.

The most important thing was to know where we were at all times, because we all had definite times over target. We might have a target time of 12:02:30. In another thirty seconds, another group might have their time over target. They would be coming from another direction to confuse the enemy gunners, so we had to be on time—not too early, and definitely not too late.

Taranto is on the heel of the Italian "boot."

Our first mission was to Saint Veit in Austria. We would fly over Italy while forming a squadron and then head over the Adriatic. We then would head north, flying over the Alps north of Yugoslavia. After we got over the Alps, we would take a heading north of Saint Veit so that when we dropped our bombs, we would be flying south and heading home. We started climbing right after takeoff. We climbed about 100 feet a minute until we got to 25,000 feet. When we went to oxygen, at 10,000 feet, we had a continuous check system with the crew to make sure everyone was OK. We had an automatic count from the nose gunner right through the whole crew to the tail gunner every ten seconds all the time we flew. Each member of the crew would call out his position, and if someone didn't answer, we checked on him immediately.

Although Powers's plane didn't have a bombardier, most B-24s, which were called "Liberators," had ten-man crews: a pilot, copilot, bombardier, navigator, radio operator, flight engineer, ball turret gunner, tail gunner and two waist gunners. The navigator sat over the nose of the plane, in front of the pilots and behind the nose gunner. The plane had four 1,200-horsepower engines, a top speed of three hundred miles per hour and a range of three thousand miles, which was more than any other American plane in World War II. Its maximum payload of eight thousand pounds was also more than any other American bomber could carry. At the same time, it was a hard plane to fly because of its stiff and heavy controls, and it quickly became known to its crews as a "flying coffin."

After we dropped our bombs and regrouped, the pilot would tell me to turn on the radio and get Foggia, which was the largest radio station the Allies had in Italy. The station came on at noon every day, and the Fifteenth Air Force dropped its bombs at noon every day. The radio station played the best and newest records from the states. So, we always flew home listening to swing music all the way. It usually was six or seven hours of flying from start to end.

Powers had been told they would be flying only every third or fourth day. But when they had a debriefing after the bombing of Saint Veit, they were told they would be flying the very next day to bomb a bridge over the Po River in northern Italy. They took off and formed their flight pattern over Rome, using the Vatican as the first turning point heading north.

When we got to the Po Valley, there was sporadic flak but nothing too heavy. There were about 200 planes altogether hitting three bridges over the river. We could actually watch our bombs land on this target, and the bridge was knocked down. We got back to debriefing, and we were really tired. We all headed for the sack. We knew we would get a couple of days' rest. But the next morning, we were awakened and told we had to go back again because the Germans had put up a pontoon bridge during the night and were crossing the river. We flew the same mission again and knocked out the pontoon bridge, but this time, we dropped bombs that had delayed action fuses so that [they] would go off at various intervals for two or three days.

On April 29, they flew a mission of close support for American ground forces in the Po Valley that were chasing the Germans right back into Germany. They blew up a train and were flying so low that the gunners had a field day firing at tanks and trucks. And then, on May 8, for the first time since they arrived in Italy, the unit members were told to appear in their class A dress uniforms. They gathered in formation at about 10:00 a.m. A jeep drove up in front of the formation, and a bird colonel got out and stood on the hood of the jeep. The squadron commander called the men to attention. The colonel took the salute from the commander and said, "Men, the war's over."

Actually, the war didn't end for Powers that day. The next morning, the commander called together Powers's crew and two crews from other squadrons. He said:

Gentlemen, we have selected you to fly today to Germany. Your planes are loaded with concentrated food and drugs for the prisoner of war camps in Germany. This is an unusual mission. You will be able to fly at any altitude your pilot selects. We want you to act as observers, and we want you to tell the navigator everything you see. You, navigators, we want you to keep complete logs. Be sure to write down the towns you fly over and what unusual things are reported to you. Have a good trip.

They took off at 7:00 a.m., and as soon as they got over the Alps, they found the roads jammed with people headed back to Germany. They were either carrying bundles or pushing various carts with their personal belongings. Every road was crowded with people—no troops or any kind of military vehicles, just ordinary people. The first town they had been told to fly over had a big airbase. All of the planes were there, but there was no one around them. "It began to dawn on us right then that maybe we were decoys to see if the Luftwaffe had really surrendered," Powers said. "They were using us as guinea pigs. When no one fired at us, they knew the war was really over. Every city that we flew over that day had an airbase, but they were all deserted. There was no sign of the military anywhere."

They finally found the POW camp, and the prisoners poured out of the buildings when they heard the engines.

We had eight large tanks of supplies in the bomb bays. They were about the size of a hot water tank. There was medicine, concentrated food, cigarettes, some newspapers, candy and a lot of vitamin pills. The pilot put down our flaps, and we were really slow flying as we came over the camp. Each tank had a parachute attached to it so it would float down instead of smashing into the ground. We saw men with crutches and slings, as well as seemingly healthy prisoners. We noticed that as soon as the tank hit the ground, a fight would seem to start over the parachute. To hell with the food. We found out later from one of our pilots who was a prisoner there that, for a parachute, you could get a woman who wanted the cloth. That was what most of them were interested in first. Food and medicine came later.

***

Powers married Bernice "Babe" Boldyga on June 16, 1945, a few days after he returned from Italy. He went to work for his father at Powers Market and was called back into service during the Koran War. Eventually, he and his wife bought the market, and they ran it until 1981. He spent most of his life in North Bennington, although, in his later years, he spent the winter months in Florida. He was a village trustee, a member of the school board and a state legislator. He was an excellent golfer and won many local tournaments, and he was a part of the group that bought Lake Paran and turned it into a community recreation area.

5

MARGARET LILLIE

Margaret Lillie, known as "Peg," was born in Bennington on January 2, 1924, and grew up in Pownal, where she, her brother and two sisters went to a one-room elementary school. She was a tiny woman with an elfin appearance. Her mother, in fact, had been born in Headford, County Galway, Ireland, which was called *Áth Cinn* in Irish. Her father had been born in East Pownal. She also was a bright and studious young woman and was a sophomore at the University of Vermont (UVM) when the war started. That in itself was unusual because Pownal didn't have a high school, and it was rare for young women from Pownal to go on to college.

By the time she graduated from UVM in 1944, there weren't many men left in the class, and many of those left were in the reserve officer training corps (ROTC). Lillie wasn't involved in the war effort in any way. "I was pretty well taken up with my studies," she later recalled. "I didn't watch for airplanes or volunteer for anything."

She had a sister working as a draftsman at Pratt & Whitney Aircraft in Hartford, Connecticut, and Lillie had worked there during the summers as a clerk, so she decided to go to Hartford to look for work. "I discovered that my BA wasn't worth very much," she said.

> *I wasn't really equipped to do anything. I couldn't type, and I had no office skills. I ended up getting a job as a psychiatric aid at the Institute for Living in Hartford. There probably wasn't anyone on the face of the earth less*

suited temperamentally for that job. It really did an awful job on me. The turnover of aides was so fast that only nine months after I started, I was the oldest aide there in terms of service.

A woman friend of Lillie's in Hartford said one day that that she was going down to the recruiting office to see about enlisting and asked Lillie to go with her. "I really had no intention of enlisting, except that I did know that I couldn't continue in that psychiatric aide job much longer. The upshot of it was that I signed up, but she didn't." She joined the WAVES (a navy unit whose formal title was "Women Accepted for Voluntary Emergency Service") and went into service one week after President Franklin Roosevelt died. "I trained at Hunter College in New York City. That was what they called 'boot camp,' and it went on for six weeks. Victory in Europe—VE Day—came while I was a seaman in boot camp. It was a hilarious time with great rejoicing."

Lillie said this of boot camp in her Bennington Historical Society interview in February 2000:

I really don't remember much about it except for the marching. I have several photographs where I'm at the end of the unit, out of step. That's not one of my fortes. You had to stand inspection: your room, your bed—that business about having the sheets so tight that they could bounce a dime off the bed. And, of course, the inspection was done with white gloves to see if there was any dust....

We had this petty officer. She was a redhead and very short and stocky. She would bark at us in these formations. It would be: "Lillie, this!" and "Lillie, that!" And, of course, she had plenty of [discipline] for me because I'm the one you can't regiment very easily. I got many demerits and did quite a bit of scrubbing those marble stairs at Hunter College because of that.

We had a very nice, very attractive navy uniform made out of worsted wool. In fact, I wore mine after I got out of the service until I wore it out. It was a skirt and a white blouse, with a black tie and a single-breasted jacket.

Opposite: Margaret "Peg" Lillie served in the WAVES and then became a lawyer and judge. *Courtesy of Margaret Lillie.*

Above: WAVES Margaret "Peg" Lillie is shown with a friend during training at Hunter College in New York. She's the woman on the left. *Courtesy of the Bennington Museum.*

After boot camp, Lillie was sent to the Naval Air Station in Atlanta, Georgia, for control tower training. She became a control tower operator and then was assigned to the Naval Air Station at Quonset Point, Rhode Island, which is now best known for the Quonset Hut, which was first manufactured there.

It was beautiful. We had a commodore who just couldn't do enough for the enlisted personnel. There was everything on that base in the way of recreation that you could possible think of....I got to be a specialist Y, second class, which was like a second-class petty officer. I was discharged towards the end of January 1947.

We could have stayed. We were given the choice to stay in the reserves. I always said that if I never had another vacation in my life, the time in the navy was like a two-year vacation. I enjoyed it immensely. We didn't go overseas. We were as far removed as anybody could be from any kind of conflict. That's why I feel a little strange when there's all this hoopla over this women's memorial in Arlington National Cemetery for all the women in service. I never felt that I was deserving of that kind of accolade. I just had a good time. I went in knowing that there were educational benefits involved. Eventually, I did go to law school on the GI Bill, which I probably never would have saved up money to do. So, really, the service was nothing but a benefit for me.

Probate Judge Margaret "Peg" Lillie. *Courtesy of the Bennington Museum.*

Lillie said that she never became very proficient at doing control tower work. So, instead of having her in the control tower itself, they would put her in a truck with a small tower on it, and her job was to watch the planes coming in to make sure they had their wheels down. If they didn't, she'd contact the tower and warn the air traffic controllers there.

Before I went into the navy, I guess I'd taken an airplane a few times from Hartford to New York City, but I hardly knew one end of a plane from the other. There were a lot of different kinds of planes by then. They'd put pictures of them on slides, and we were supposed to identify all these different types of planes, like identifying birds by their shapes and sizes. That was all brand new to me, and I never got that good at it.

After being discharged in 1947, Lillie went back home and took a job at Bennington College. But her goal was to become a lawyer, and her time in the service qualified her for GI Bill benefits that would pay for three years at Boston College Law School. "They not only paid tuition, but they paid room and board. It wasn't very generous, but it was enough to get by on."

***

PEG LILLIE BECAME ONE of the few female lawyers in the state in 1953, and eventually, she served as both a probate judge and as the Bennington County state's attorney.

6

LEONARD MORRISON

Much of what we know about Bennington during World War II came from a local attorney named Leonard W. Morrison, a remarkable person in many ways. He was thirty-four years old at the time of the attack on Pearl Harbor, balding and bespectacled and very much overweight. A lifelong bachelor, he also had a bad heart and other ailments, but nonetheless, he made the trip to the recruiting center in Rutland, where he tried to enlist in the army. Bill Kearns said that the army doctors "took one look at him and told him to go back home and not waste any more of his own time or theirs."

Morrison had been born in Maynard, Massachusetts, on April 9, 1907, and ended up in Bennington on March 31, 1930, when his father, a spinner, took a job in one of the mills. He had been born with a defective heart, and once, as a child, he had overheard his doctor telling his mother that he probably wouldn't live another year. While his younger brother, Donald, was a good athlete, playing football and baseball at Bennington High School, Leonard had a sheltered childhood. He was seldom allowed out of the house when he was young, and, instead, he was kept indoors, playing the piano and becoming a voracious reader. He would become an accomplished pianist, whose repertoire ranged from Mozart and Bach to the show tunes of Rogers and Hart. He was a studious young man who spent much of his time reading Shelly, Keats, Byron, Milton and Shakespeare. He graduated from the Massachusetts Agricultural College (now the University of Massachusetts at Amherst) and studied law in the Bennington firm headed by Francis Morrissey. That was during a time when someone could still become a lawyer without going to law school—they would read law in an established law firm and then pass the bar exam. Before that, Morrison had been a reporter for the *Bennington Banner*, and eventually, he became a part-owner of the Bennington Bookstore.

Frustrated at not being able to join the army, Morrison went to his former employer Frank "Ginger" Howe, the publisher of the *Bennington Banner*, with a proposal that he would write a weekly column for the newspaper every Friday that would have the dual purpose of telling the people who were still in Bennington what was happening to the town's men and women in the service and telling Bennington people in the service what was happening in the town. The column would be called "Letter from Home," and people in Bennington could clip it from the

Leonard W. Morrison. Photograph courtesy of the Bennington Banner.

Leonard Morrison wrote the "Letter from Home" columns throughout the war years. *Courtesy of the* Bennington Banner.

newspaper and include it in their own letters to friends and relatives in the service. Morrison's letters were much like those that an uncle in Bennington might write to a favored nephew in a foxhole in Italy, mixing news about local politics, local food rationing and high school sports with news about Bennington service people who had been promoted, transferred, decorated, wounded or killed. They managed to mix humor and poignancy in ways that were not at all awkward, and they managed to seamlessly combine news about Bennington men killed in bomber crashes in France with news about missed foul shots in high school basketball games. They were lively and engaging and showed in vivid ways just how a small town in Vermont was being impacted by the war.

"I loved them," said Larry Powers, whose parents sent them to him every week. "Sometimes, it would take them two weeks to catch up to me, but I looked forward to getting them." When he did, Powers—along with other Bennington men and women all over the world, even in POW camps—could learn that "Lewis Carpenter is on his way home from the European front after having been wounded, captured, imprisoned, hospitalized and released"; that "J. Lawrence Bradley, who saw service in the First World War and who is seabeeing his way through this one, has a Purple Heart for a wound received in the North African campaign"; and that "Dr. Francis C. Tomasi, Bennington dentist, has been made a captain in the air force." They would learn that "Staff Sgt. J. Clement Marcoux, who is having a medical furlough home, gave a speech to the Lions during the week, got feted at a party and then got himself wedded to a girl from Hoosick Falls, Miss Agnes French"; that "Tubby" Austin, "who is in the European theater, has received a certificate of merit for gallantry with the armored infantry"; that "the fishing has been stinking so far this year"; that "Lt. Louis Graves, after having been captured by the Germans, is now safe in an Army hospital after a thrilling rescue"; and that "it was 44 below zero in Woodford one morning last week." They would learn that "Ray Harrington, prisoner of the Germans, has been liberated"; that "Norman Rockwell's oldest boy, Jerry, is at the hospital with a fractured skull having been beaned by a baseball while playing on the Arlington village green"; that "Marine Private J.B. (Punchy) Beaulieu and Marie Rose Ottaviano have been married"; that "Staff Sergeant Edward J. Knapp Jr., waist gunner on a Flying Fortress who was reported missing in action is now known to be safe and in good hands"; that "a scrap drive is underway in Bennington with the slogan, 'A piece of scrap for every Jap'"; and that "Sgt. Donald E. White of North Bennington was in the crew of the first American bomber over Berlin." They would learn that "Pvt. Herbert Hill of Burgess Road was killed in action in Italy....His brother, Robert Hill, was killed last July in the South Pacific"; that "football, of course, is in the wind...and the opening game will see the team sparked by Darrell (Squirrel) Sawyer who weighs 103 pounds soaking wet"; that "Lorayne Fehily has fashioned a baptismal gown for her baby out of a parachute once used by her husband who is now overseas"; that "Captain Robert A. Sausville has been awarded the Distinguished Flying Cross"; that Virginia Peer Brougham, "whose Marine husband, Pfc. Edward Brougham," had been killed in the Pacific had joined the Women's Army Corps; and that Earl Alderman of Stark Street had become the first Benningtonian to donate a gallon of blood to the Red Cross. They would learn that Lieutenant George Slater Jr., the son of the music director of the Bennington High School band, had been killed in Europe; that there would be a good many more shades drawn in the village if "the more modest among the populace suspected the power and accuracy of the binoculars" being used by the civilian airplane spotters on a hillside; that "Tech. Sgt. Lawrence E. LaFlamme, radio gunner of a Flying Fortress and a veteran of 50 combat missions with the 15th AAF in Italy is home on furlough"; that "Miss Frances Mooney and Miss Madalyn Wills of the Putnam Memorial Hospital staff have signed up for army nursing service"; and that "a memorial service will be held Sunday at St. Peter's Church for the repose of the soul of Lt. William A. Root, who was killed in action in Germany."

Left: The officer is Lieutenant Francis Tomasi. He was an army dentist, and the picture was taken in 1943 at the U.S. Army Air Corps Hospital in Bryan, Texas. *Courtesy of the Bennington Museum.*

Right: First Lieutenant William A. Root III is shown in an army dress uniform, standing next to a low wall. *Courtesy of the Bennington Museum.*

Morrison also set about collecting pictures of Bennington men and women in the service, many of which ended up in the archives of the Bennington Museum. Today, they help us to match faces to the names in Morrison's columns and, thus, add to the sense that we have of Bennington in the war. They include snapshots of Carl "Curley" Williams, the Ben-Hi (Bennington High School) basketball coach who was serving with the Seventh Armored Division in Europe; Marine Lieutenant Robert Ryan and his navy pharmacist mate brother, William, posed in white summer uniforms in front of their family home at 334 School Street; Gedeon LaCroix on Iwo Jima; and Private William F. Gordon sitting on a low wire fence with mountains in the background, seemingly as happy and relaxed as a grasshopper on a blade of grass. He would later be killed in action on December 22, 1944, in St. Vith, Belgium, during the Battle of the Bulge.

Left: Second Lieutenant Louis G. Graves is shown in a winter uniform, standing in a snowy field. He was captured by the Germans, wounded and rescued. *Courtesy of the Bennington Museum.*

Right: Darrell Sawyer Jr. is shown in his leather flying suit. *Courtesy of the Bennington Museum.*

The images show Lillian Dougherty in her navy WAVES uniform; Lieutenant John Bernard Hart, the first baby born at Putnam Memorial Hospital, in his army uniform; and Seaman Sterling Wilson in his navy uniform. Wilson would come home to marry his Bennington sweetheart and Bennington College graduate Polly Ridlon. They also show Sergeant Charles Del Tatto, whose father had been one of the Italian stone masons brought to Bennington to build the Everett Estate and who had written to Morrison to say how thrilled he was that his photography unit had filmed the dropping of the atomic bomb on Hiroshima.

Morrison was well-liked in Bennington, where he livened up many gatherings with his engaging public speaking and his piano playing. He also wrote a good deal of poetry, although some of it was more like doggerel, and this also made its way into many of his "Letter from Home" columns. For example, there was this parody of "A Visit from St. Nicholas" that complained about the gas rationing that was imposed by

Clockwise from top left: Portrait of Lillian Docherty in her WAVES uniform; Sterling Wilson is shown in his navy uniform; Portrait of Private First Class Charles Del Tatto in his United States Army Air Corps uniform; Lieutenant John Bernard Harte is shown in his army uniform with a Sam Brown Belt. *Images courtesy of the Bennington Museum.*

former secretary of the interior Harold Ickes, who had been charged by President Roosevelt with overseeing petroleum production and rationing to meet wartime needs.

> *It's the night before Christmas,*
> *and all through the land,*
> *Not a creature is stirring,*
> *for gas has been banned.*
> *The tires are hung by the fire*
> *with care.*
> *The garage isn't safe*
> *since crude rubber got rare.*
> *The children all snuggled down tight*
> *in their beds*
> *With visions of sugar and gas*
> *in their heads.*
> *And Daddy and Mom have to*
> *stay in the house*
> *'Cause Ickes has cancelled*
> *their gas cards, the louse.*

Or this, from another column:

> *Winter must be on the way*
> *'Cause we got coal the other day.*
> *It swizzled down the metal chute*
> *As black as Daddy's Sunday suit.*

> *That night when Daddy saw the bill,*
> *Somehow, he seemed to get quite ill.*

Morrison's style was that of a storyteller, not a historian. But in ways that were often folksy and sometimes poignant, he told people in the service what was happening in Bennington and told people in Bennington what was happening to their men and women in the service. The result was to provide much of the raw material for a history of Bennington in the war, as these excerpts from various columns show:

September 18, 1942:

Saddest of any news that has come to Bennington since the beginning of the war was the notification received by Mr. and Mrs. John J. Leahy of Putnam Street that their son, Jack, has been reported missing September 5 in the North American theater. It was only a matter of ten days ago or so prior to receiving this notification that Jack had piloted an army bomber over Main Street....Equally disturbing was the official message from the War Department that Harold Francis Littlefield, son of Mrs. Harry Harbour of Beech Street, had been killed in action with the United States Navy....And among the best news of the week is the notification that Andy Maloney has been promoted to the rank of captain. Andy went south with the national guard, and it speaks well for the kind of job he is doing that his advancement has been so consistent.

January 2, 1943:

Christmas Eve on Parris Island was not the Christmas of snowy vistas—of trees standing naked against glowering skies or the sharp shoulders of Walloomsac hills pressing raggedly upon dark storm

John T. Leahy, a pilot who was killed when his plane crashed, shown in his summer uniform. *Courtesy of the Bennington Museum.*

clouds. It was warm down there in South Carolina, and throughout the day, the "boots" had sweated and steamed under the rigid drilling of their instructors. When the day was done and the soft southern night had fallen, weary boys dragged themselves to their bunks to rest and write home. By some chance, the Kinney boys, "Faucet" and Jim, met Jackie Kearns. And the trio looked about for others from home. So, on Christmas Eve, a thousand miles away, some kids from Bennington forgot their aching feet and lame backs. Jackie Kearns, the Kinney brothers, Art Patten, Herm LeRay, Junior Kelson and Johnny Howard spent the evening together. Just as if they were a curbstone group in front of the Paradise restaurant, they kidded and crabbed. Their conversation wasn't at all about the halls of Montezuma or the shores of Tripoli. Not once during the night did they stray from Bennington. When the taps sounded, they went their separate ways. On the morrow, they began again their lessons in crawling 100 yards on their bellies, pulling themselves along by their elbows, carrying their rifles and cartridges, never exposing an inch of their torsos to slant-eyed snipers. On the morrow, they went back again to the maneuvering and eternal back-breaking drill. But for the night before Christmas, they moved Putnam Square to Parris Island. It made everything all right.

March 31, 1944:

Signs of spring: Green grass on the post office lawn; bright new hats on all the maiden-lady office workers; ladders on a roof as shingling begins; two kids sailing a beautiful big ship in a beautiful puddle; the young lad coming up River Street Sunday with a fielder's glove in his hand; 15 boys roosting like crows on the steps of the Methodist church Saturday; water furrows on every lawn in town.

June 15, 1944:

Bud Dewey (Charles H.) is stationed with an embarkation unit in an eastern seaboard city. The city can't be named because of the Banner's *ideas about giving away military intelligence to the enemy....So, without saying where Bud Dewey is, it should be noted that he is walking on terrain which was purchased from the Indians for 24 smackers and a bottle of firewater and it was governed by the Dutch before the Irish got all the soft political jobs, the Jews bought all the buildings, and the Greeks managed all the restaurants. It has the highest buildings, the highest prices and the highest dresses in the world.*

October 27, 1944:

Apples crowd every roadside stand from here to Canada. Northern Spies and Mackintosh seem to be favorites, although baskets of Greenings are plentiful, and an occasional showing of Russets is to be found. The usual price is $3.95 or $4.00 per bushel. Only in the valleys are there still brightly colored maples or beeches to be seen. The hills are brown and sere. Rains over the weekend swept the last of the hillside colors to the ground. The air is filled with frost, sneezes and snuffling. Winter is on its way.

March 2, 1945

Seaman 2C Elmer Harrington and Ship's Cook William Cobleigh, who didn't know each other existed before they left Bennington, are now buddies somewhere in the Pacific....Cpl. Edward H. Myers has been wounded in Germany....Sgt. Truman Noyes has been awarded the Silver Star for gallantry in action in Italy....Staff Sgt. Ray LeBlanc was wounded on Luzon and his brother, Pfc. Henry LaBlanc is in this country having been wounded in Germany...the 1945 registration plates have begun to arrive.

April 13, 1945

Today is Friday the 13ᵗʰ, by superstitious people thought to be a day of ill luck. We all hope it will be so for certain leaders in this world who never realized that so many fellows and gals from a little town they never heard of were willing to travel so far and work so hard and do such a job just to keep that town safe and what they wanted it to be. Hitler and Hirohito and their ilk never knew how much the people of Bennington, the boys and girls, their folks and their friends, were willing to endure to keep from being pushed around. On this day, the gangsters' luck seems to be running out, the boys are nipping closer to Nippon and the western front is getting as close to Berlin, Germany, as our own West Road is to Berlin, New York. The war, in fact, looks so good that we are hearing talk of V-Day celebrations, and some are even talking of building some sort of war memorial for the veterans of all wars. It seems not a bad idea but very, very premature with the largest group of fighting men that ever left town for any war and probably more than went to all the other wars combined still away from home without a voice in the plan.

From past experience in war memorials, we should go slowly and with care. In its one monument, Bennington has been very fortunate: our monument, for sheer, simple beauty, inspiring stability and enduring grandeur, is unique. Some towns, however, have gotten many things they neither wanted nor needed—the monstrosities of piles of boulders topped off by stacks of muskets that were erected in many village squares after the Civil War are the

Private Truman A. Noyes wearing an army dress uniform. *Courtesy of the Bennington Museum.*

chief offenders. The Rough Riders of the War with Spain inspired equestrian creations that most of the then-youthful thought were in honor of Bill Hart. (Editor's Note: William Hart was a silent film star who appeared mainly in Westerns and was a friend of Wyatt Earp and Bat Masterson. His films were known for authentic costumes and props, and he rode a brown and white pinto in them that was called "Fritz.") Recently, there were the many captured tanks and Big Berthas of World War I, which, ironically, went back to war as scrap iron. Consider the millions and billions that have been wasted in this war that could have been used to do so many needed, beautiful and wonderful things. It seems that when we plan a memorial to those who fought for a "lasting peace," we should strive to make up for that waste and make sure it will be something that will truly serve and is truly needed in a needing world.

June 15, 1945

The American passion for interposing rules and regulations on common sense propositions is, once again, demonstrated in the matter of the GI Bill of Rights. Most of us who had supposed that a discharged soldier could automatically get a $2,000 loan from the government for building his home have been somewhat numbed to learn the restrictions on which the bureaucrats are imposing on the law. First stupidity, which ought to be obvious to anyone familiar with Bennington's screwy listing system: loans cannot exceed the valuation of the property. In Bennington, we list at one-third the valuation. Result, the poor soldier gets nicked. Second stupidity: the soldier must have had a good business record before going into the service. Where does that leave some of the youngsters who went with Company I, who were just out of school and never had a better job than mowing lawns? Third stupidity: In business matters, the loan is only for equipment and not for merchandise with which to get started. The answer? Let's pepper Messrs. Austin, Aiken and Plumley (Editor's Note: Warren Austin, George Aiken and Charles Plumley were Vermont's two U.S. Senators and one House member) with notes and letters and telegrams. They just gave themselves an expense account of $2,500 a year. They ought to be willing to do something for a fugitive from a foxhole.

An example of how he brought everything together can be seen in this "Letter from Home" column from Friday, October 6, 1944, which is being reprinted here in just as it appeared in the *Bennington Banner*:

"Discomfort"

Solitary, in the night,
I hear a single fly,
Buzzing round with all his might
About my tight-shut eye.

His friends have disappeared for
  good
And, sleepily, I wish he would.

Bombers burping through the autumn night kept the breezes fanned all through the week. They skidded over Bennington in droves, giving the home folks a chance to chat about the new air armada, which is being assembled for V-Day. One morning during the week, there was a skittish fellow who spent half an hour or so loping from the sun towards the courthouse and performing all the tricks which the air corps has thought of outlawing for the benefit of the gaping ganders along our main business artery.

***

The high school football team, having lost to Drury by a single touchdown in the first game of the season, defeated Williamstown last week by a 13–6 score, although outweighed at least 15 pounds to the man. The team showed a zest and zip which made the eyes of the onlookers goggle. Without benefit of stars, the outfit worked together as a well-disciplined unit and, even when the going was tough, dug to put up a surprising battle. Williamstown's score was made in the final quarter against the second team when the game was well on ice. Comment in general was that the aggregation is the best looking grid squad the high school has had since 1933, and unless their hairlines get too big for their hatbands, the lads ought to do well during the coming weeks.

***

Harry Conley was killed in a plane crash in France, according to word received this week by his wife, Mrs. Barbara Gardner Conley. Harry was overseas in the employee of Pratt & Whitney, supervising work on airplane motors. He had been in Africa, Corsica and had advanced into France with the victorious push of the American forces after the landings at Toulon.

***

Time *magazine carried a haloed photo of Mary Spargo, former* Banner *reporter, who is employed in Washington by the* Washington Post *with the following comment:*

"The Washington Post, *last week, printed a sensational report that started a great cackling among Washington news hens. According to the report, there is a secret list which Capitol Hill's 135 female reporters are supposed to keep of U.S. senators and representatives 'to stay on the other side of the desk from.' Added to the prominent names on the list were such descriptive names as 'Garter Snapper,' 'Revolving-Door Romeo (he gets into the same compartment of a revolving door and pinches), 'Elevator Lothario,' 'Gooser Gander,' and 'Desk Athlete' (he jumps).*

Almost to a woman, the Washington women's press corps uprose in indignation. They declared that had never seen or heard of such a list, swore that few Congressmen are less than perfect gentlemen, said the articles had made their work harder by making Congressmen afraid to be alone with them. They were even more curious than indignant when the author of the unsigned stories turned out to be plump, bespectacled Post *reporter Mary Spargo, a one-time investigator for the Dies Committee."*

***

Almost daily, as you thumb through the papers reading of the European war, you note news dispatches from Robert C. Wilson of Grove Street, war correspondent holding the rank of captain with the Canadian army and covering the Allied struggle towards the tip of the British salient in the Netherlands on the south bank of the Neder Rhine, south of Rankum.

***

Miss Jean E. Baker, daughter of Mr. and Mrs. Frank W. Baker of Hicks Corners, has been sworn into the WAC.... The pheasant season has opened and the woods, and brush, from now on, be filled with hunters and bird shot.... The Elks drive to raise money for the purchase of their new home is swooping along in high gear.... Thirty-seven members of the Banner *gang and their wives and children attended a picnic at the South Stream Maison of Kurt Hoffman to celebrate the 74th birthday of Frank E. Howe.... Donald Turner, 22-year-old North Bennington turkey farmer, died by suffocation late Saturday afternoon in a sawdust silo at the Warner Brush Manufacturing Company on Main Street. The young man had taken his farm truck to the plant to get a load of sawdust and had entered the silo to make the sawdust flow more freely. It cascaded about him, and he was buried so deeply, it was five or ten minutes before he could be extricated.*

***

Lt. Richard A. Fonteneau, pilot of a Flying Fortress with the 15th Army Air Force in Italy and, until recently, a war prisoner in Romania; Lt. Frederick L. Dunn, pilot of a Liberator in France and Italy; Staff Sgt. Earl A. Malon, waist gunner on a Fortress and veteran of 51 missions—including the first shuttle mission from Italy to Russia; and Staff Sgt. Edward Silver, who has 67 bombing missions noted down in his mem-book, are all home on leave.

***

Rev. G. A. Heald of Woodstock, Vt., will be the new rector of St. Peter's Episcopal Church to succeed the Rev. Parker C. Webb, who recently resigned to become a member of the faculty of an Episcopal school in Kenosha, Wis.…William F. Moore, probably the smoothest guard any Bennington High School basketball team ever had, has opened the restaurant and filling station on the Troy Road formerly known as White's Station and just across the New York state line.…Four were hurt when a sedan driven by Francis Dragon, petty officer 3c., U.S. Navy, skidded on a wet pavement on Washington Avenue in Albany.

***

"Solitude"

The sun is warm upon the hills today,
And there is smoky fragrance to the air.
In fields, the corn is stacked the
   ancient way,
Like wigwams built for braves
   no longer there.

By noon, there are no filmy veils
  of frost
Lying with pallid grace across the
  land,
And leaves which autumn winds
  have gaily tossed
Like brown foam lie within the
  maple stand.
The bluejay's velvet wing is not so
  blue
At husking time when twilight
  cloaks the world.
The beech and birch sift darkening
  shadows through
Curled fingers—like small banners
  neatly furled.
Such beauty, without you to share
  with me
Brings pain to where my heart
  should be.

***

Johnny Behan has opened the gas station at the corner of Dewey and Main Streets....The Banner *carried this week a photograph showing the blazing gasoline tank truck in which Frank E. Nason, young Benningtonian, was imprisoned by flame in the crushed cab and burned to death....Samuel Margolin has re-elected president of the Bennington Hebrew congregation....Nick Carbonaro says that black woodchucks aren't as scarce as us home-haunting hunters had thought. He has pictures of one killed in 1942 by his son, Nick Jr., who is now somewhere in the Philippines knocking off little yellow chipmunks. Nick also says that he knows where there is another coal black woodchuck, which emerges daily to chin chummily with neighbors on East Road.*

***

Staff Sgt. Charles L. Harrington, U.S. Army Ranger, has been wounded in action somewhere in France....Mrs. Margaret Price, mother of Pfc.

Charles H. Wheeler, who died of typhus last August in New Guinea, has a letter of condolence from Gen. Douglas McArthur....Tech. Sgt. Lawrence E. LaFlamme, radio gunner on a Flying Fortress and veteran of 50 combat missions with the 15th AAF in Italy is home on furlough. Incidentally, LaFlamme and Earl Malon were close enough together in Italy to swap doughnuts daily. Malon set out for the states 15 days ahead of LaFlamme, and LaFlamme got home one day before Malon. Earl came over on a boat that had the speed of a limping stork while Lawrence skimmed the skyways.

***

Pfc. Milton D. Hall of Wilmington was killed in action in France on August 28....Pfc. LeRoy Becker has the Purple Heart as a result of wounds received in France....Mrs. Catherine Dumas of River Street, listening to the radio last Friday, got startled nearly out of her stays when she heard the radio announcer from somewhere inside the German border say that among the soldiers standing near him was Sgt. Harold Sausville, youngest son of Mrs. Edward Sausville Sr. of River Street. Sgt. Harold has been in Africa and Sicily. For a while, he was in England and, since D-Day, has been harrying the Huns in France.

***

Pfc. Wallace L. Mattison Jr., son of Fire Chief and Mrs. Mattison of East Main Street, was seriously wounded in action in France on September 12....Alfred T. Morrill, former secretary of the local "Y" and more recently state secretary for the state YMCA organization, has resigned his job to further his work with the USO....Dick McGurn and Francis Kervan met recently somewhere in England. Francis, who is known as "Fat" because of his blimp-like profile, took Richard to the small town where Kervan had been stationed for some months. According to the letter McGurn wrote home, Francis practically has the place in his pocket. "Hello, Charley," he said to an elderly gaffer caning his way along the street. "Who is that?" asked Richard. "Oh," said Fat. "He's Lord Blankinhere. He's a duke or something. He owns this place. We're good pals."

***

Al Smith is dead. It's 16 years since he campaigned for the presidency and got defeated by the vote that split the solid South. He was not, perhaps, a great man in the sense that Lincoln and Jackson were great, but he came very close to the mark. And if he missed it, it was because of his loyalties to lesser men. Chesterton would have said, though, that such a loss was his greatest gain. "When you're leading a parade," Al once said to some of his cocksure assistants, "look around to make sure it hasn't turned down a side street."

***

"Falling Leaves"

First, the hills are red and gold,
And then they're drab and brown.
Quite suddenly, the trees look old
As you go 'round the town.

And soon, the kids are wading thru
The dry and crackling mounds,
While those who raked the dry
*   leaves view,*
With ire, their joyous sounds.

Each night, a pall of smoke will lie
(Like cream upon mustaches)
Across the town while husbands try
To burn the leaves to ashes.

And then the village board will
*   meet*
And sound a warning note:
"Please have no fires on any street
That has an asphalt coat."

"It was a very popular column and very well read," Kearns said many years later. "It was his way of contributing to the war effort. He was very proud of it and justly so." The publisher of a competing paper, the *Rutland Herald*, agreed, writing, "If and when citations are handed out to home front columnists for morale building, the accolade in Vermont should go to Morrison of the *Bennington Banner*."

***

MORRISON WAS ADMIRED AND respected for his personal generosity, for the great amount of pro bono legal work that he did and for his efforts in helping young people like Kearns improve their lives. He was elected village attorney in 1941 and to the Vermont legislature in 1944, 1946 and 1948, but he had to resign in 1949, when he developed tuberculosis in addition to his heart problems and couldn't attend the legislative session. But while he was in the legislature, he had worked closely with Republican governor Ernest W. Gibson Jr. to develop Democratic support for a tax reform plan that Gibson—a progressive Republican—was intent on turning into law despite opposition from the more conservative members of the Republican Party. Morrison helped draft the bill and then became a leading advocate of it, speaking passionately in favor of it on the floor of the House. Gibson was so impressed with Morrison that he appointed him commissioner of taxes in 1949, despite the fact that he was a Democrat (and, at the time, Democrats headed no departments in state government), and despite the fact that, because of his tuberculosis, he was confined to the Vermont Sanitarium in Pittsford at the time. Gibson had cleared the appointment in advance with the head of the sanitarium and, according to Kearns, had told Morrison in a phone conversation that he was giving him the job to just do as much work as he could whenever he was well enough to do it.

According to the *Bennington Banner*, there were many who thought that Morrison was not only one of the brightest people in state government in the 1940s and early 1950s but had everything needed to become governor except for good health and the right party affiliation. Not only had Vermont not elected a Democrat as governor since before the Civil War, but there were very few Democrats occupying full-time jobs anywhere in state government. Morrison and Kearns, in fact, were two of the very few who listed themselves as Democrats in the annual legislative directory. There were others on the payroll, but they generally—and perhaps prudently—tended to list themselves as Independents.

He eventually became a superior court judge and was finally done in by his lifelong heart problems. He died suddenly of a heart attack in Bennington when he was just fifty-five years old.

7

JOHN MALONEY

John Maloney spent the war with the Ninth Infantry Division, serving in Africa, Sicily, France, Belgium and Germany. The Ninth Division—known both as the "Old Reliables" and the "Notorious Ninth"—was one of the first U.S. units to engage in combat in World War II. In all, it spent 264 days in combat and suffered more than 3,800 killed and more than 17,000 wounded. It was the first American infantry division to fight its way into Germany in September 1944, and then—on March 7, 1945—it was the first to cross the Rhine River using the "Ludendorff Bridge" near Remagen, which was the only bridge over the Rhine that the Germans hadn't managed to destroy. The Ludendorff had also been wired for demolition, but the Ninth fought its way across it before the Germans could detonate the charges. "We had the misfortune or the good fortune to go in first," Maloney recalled in February 2000. His division was the first infantry unit to fight its way over the Rhine since the Napoleonic Wars.

Maloney was born in Bennington in 1917, the third boy in a family that ended up with eight boys and three girls. Five of the eight sons ended up in World War II, serving in the army, the air corps and the navy. "It went well. None of us got killed," Maloney recalled. "I was one of the fortunate ones to go through without anything happening to me." He attended the St. Francis de Sales Elementary School and graduated from Bennington High School in 1935. Although he grew up in Bennington, he left home early and spent several years riding the rails during the Great Depression. "I used to ride the freight trains. I traveled a lot, all over the country, for three or four years. My family, with all them kids and everything, it helped to have one less mouth to feed."

Maloney tried to enlist right after the attack on Pearl Harbor but was rejected because of a malocclusion. He was later drafted in July 1942, and this time, he was taken despite his overbite. There was only one other person from Bennington in his division he knew of. That was Vernet Houran, who was badly wounded and sent home, but he survived his wounds and lived to be seventy-five years old.

Maloney did his basic training at Fort Bragg, became a military policeman (MP) and landed at Casablanca in December 1942. He took part in the Battle of Kasserine Pass

John Maloney. *Courtesy of the Maloney family.*

in Tunisia, where the Americans were badly defeated by General Erwin Rommel and his Afrika Korps. That was the battle that caused a major shake-up in American leadership and caused General George Patton to be moved into a leadership role. Maloney was with the Ninth Division when it fought its way from Morocco back into Tunisia in late March 1943 and captured Bizerte in early May. One American unit that followed the French Foreign Legion troops into Bizerte had soldiers in a Jeep holding up a busty mannequin they had liberated from a lingerie shop, singing a new barracks ballad that would eventually have more than two hundred verses, all of them salacious. It began:

> *Dirty Gertie from Bizerte*
> *Hid a mousetrap 'neath her skirtie.*
> *Made her boyfriend's finger hurtie…*

From then until August 1943, Maloney and the Ninth Division remained near Oran, Morocco, until they invaded Sicily on August 9. When asked what he remembered most about the invasion, Maloney answered, "That I managed to stay alive."

In November of that year, his unit went to England, where it was based in Winchester until just before D-Day. It was actually June 9, three days after the initial D-Day landings, when Maloney's unit landed at Utah Beach. "We couldn't land [on D-Day itself] on account of the harbor all being clogged up with sunken boats and everything else. There was no place to land." When they did land, they moved on to Cherbourg, where they helped capture that important port city and then took part in the heavy fighting that led to the capture of Saint Lô, or the ruins that were left of it after heavy bombing by Americans.

The 9th Division was already near Aachen, Germany, where Charlemagne held court and is buried, when it raced back into Belgium to help stop the Germans at the Battle of the Bulge, which Maloney described as "terrible" fighting. He said he admired the way that General Anthony McAuliff, whose 101st Airborne Division was completely encircled by German forces, replied to a demand that he surrender—a one-word response that said, "Nuts."

The end result was that Maloney took part in many more battles than most Bennington servicemen and survived them without a scratch, although he seems to have had nightmares after being discharged in September 1945. "There were a lot of bad nights," he later recalled. "I had malaria over there, and I had a couple of relapses of that. Otherwise, I guess I was one of the lucky ones."

***

MALONEY RETURNED TO BENNINGTON and married Martina LaRoche, who had been working in one of the local mills. They had a son and two daughters. He went from being an MP in the army to being an officer in the local police force, where he served for two years. He was elected Bennington County sheriff in 1947, and he held that job until he retired in 1986. He was a member of the Elks Club, the Knights of Columbus, the American Legion and Veterans of Foreign Wars, the Loyal Order of Moose and the local country club. He was eighty-eight years old when he died in 2005.

8

ROBERT PURDY

When Robert Purdy was drafted into the service on November 4, 1944, he was twenty-eight years old and married with two children. He also had a younger brother, Kenneth, who had gone off to war with Bennington's Company I of the Vermont National Guard and had been killed in the South Pacific the previous September. Purdy was working at Benmont Papers at the time, and because it was doing some government work, his boss told him that he could probably get him a deferment. "Don't try, because all my buddies have gone, and I want to go," Purdy told him. He later told the Bennington Historical Society that his wife hadn't been happy about his decision.

Purdy had been born in Pittsfield, Massachusetts, on December 2, 1917, and raised in Pownal, where he had gone to the one-room Maple Grove School. His father had been born in Boston to parents from Ireland and Scotland and had been given up for adoption because there were so many children in the family that his parents couldn't feed and clothe them. He was adopted by Andrew and Sophia Maurer, a brother-and-sister pair who lived in Bennington, and he went by Richard Maurer until he married Purdy's mother, Mildred Hicks of Pownal, and took back his original name of Richard Purdy. He was killed in a motorcycle accident in Brattleboro when Robert Purdy was just three years old.

Purdy did his basic training at Fort McClellan, Alabama. "The training was good. They had good food. A lot of people complained about the food, of course, but being brought up on the farm, I wasn't fussy about food. We ate what we had on the farm, so when I went down there in basic training, I ate what they put on the table. It was all good, healthy food." When he finished basic training, he volunteered for paratroop training—not because he wanted to jump out of airplanes, but because he needed the money.

Robert Purdy. *Courtesy of the Purdy family.*

> *I was married and had the two children. My first paycheck* [from basic training] *was something like twelve dollars and a few cents. And I said, "I've got to have more money than this." Of course, you don't need much when you're in the army, but I wanted more. I saw a big sign on the wall that said, "Join the parachute infantry and get fifty dollars more." So, I had to sign up for it because I needed the fifty dollars more, and they sent me to Fort Benning, Georgia, to do the parachute school.*

Army privates, at the time, had a base pay of fifty dollars a month, but paratroopers got an additional fifty dollars a month.

Purdy had no problems with basic training, but training to be a paratrooper was a different story. "That was rugged. I was in a company of kids. I'm twenty-eight years old, and all these other guys are eighteen- and nineteen-year-old kids. I had to work hard to stay with them guys. It does make a difference, ten years. But I did good. I thought I did good for my age and everything, because a lot of them didn't pass, and I did."

The following excerpt is from an interview Purdy did with the historical society on February 2, 2000.

> Interviewer. *What did it feel like when you jumped?*
> Purdy. *Just like stepping out into the air. It was nothing to it.*
> Interviewer. *The temperature wasn't extreme?*
> Purdy. *No. The wind was blowing by you from the airplane. They fly about one hundred miles an hour, so you would feel the blast from the props.*
> Interviewer. *Was it exciting to look down from that first jump and see the ground?*
> Purdy. *No, you didn't pay too much attention to it. As I remember, you go out the door, and you feel the 'chute open up, and you look up to make sure it's all right. Then you look around to see where all the rest of your buddies*

are. You can steer your 'chute a little bit, so if you saw John Doe over there, you would try to get over to where he was so you could land with him or near him. Then you made sure nothing was under you. If there was a bunch of trees, you'd try to get away from them. You could steer the 'chute a little bit, but of course, the wind could make you drift something wicked.

Interviewer. *To what outfit were you assigned?*

Purdy. *After the parachute school, I went to communication school. All the guys that went through parachute school with me and learned to jump—shortly afterwards, they were in the Battle of the Bulge. But the day we graduated, a sergeant said to me something about going to communications school. I said, "Well, what's that all about?" And he told me it's about eleven weeks training and said he thought I'd be good at it. So, I went to this communications school* [instead of going overseas with] *most of the guys I had trained with. Most of them were at the Battle of the Bulge, and most of them got wiped out. But I had that eleven weeks of communications school, and that made me stay in the states a lot longer. Then when I got through with that, I went to advanced infantry training, and that was another two weeks.*

Interviewer. *Was that training preparing you to be a radioman?*

Purdy. *I couldn't be a radioman too well because I couldn't learn the Morse code. I had an awful time with it. We had communications lines, wire lines, we got to set up in different places. We used to do all these different problems, like they'd set up a command post and* [have us] *run lines from this command post to the next one, and it all had to be done in the dark.*

One night, just before dark, they put a whole bunch of us on an airplane and took us down to the Gulf of Mexico. There was a little island there that they said was about a half mile wide and four miles long. They dumped us off. Some of us landed on the island, and some landed in the ocean because the wind was blowing awful hard. Then we had to dig a little hole and wait until it got dark. Then everybody had to meet in a certain spot, and we were given compass bearings and told where to go. We were told to string wires from here to there, and if it was anywhere people would be walking, we had to string them up where they wouldn't be running into them or bury them. We spent most of the night at it and then reassembled in the morning. They went around and inspected everything to make sure we'd done it right. Then they put us on a boat and took us to the mainland and put us back on a plane to Fort Benning. The guys that went and took down the wires that we had put up the night before said I had tied the wires to every poison oak tree on the island. If you could see me the next day, you would think so. I was just one mass of it. My hands were covered. My face was covered. So, I had to go to the medics, and they put me in the hospital for a little while until I got rid of it.

After Purdy left Fort Benning, he was assigned to the Eleventh Airborne, which was in the Pacific. He first was given a thirty-day furlough and came home to Bennington before taking a train to Fort Ord in California to ship out for the Pacific. He was on the train when the atom bombs were dropped on Hiroshima and Nagasaki and was on a ship moving under the Golden Gate Bridge when word came over the radio that Japan had surrendered.

When we left Fort Ord, they gave us wool clothes. Now, this was in summertime, so we assumed we were headed for Alaska. Then, the first thing we know, we're crossing the equator, going south. Then we got to the Marshall Islands, which is way south. Then we went from there to the Philippines. The morning we entered Manila Harbor, you never saw so many wool clothes floating on the water. Everybody was just throwing them overboard, because they knew they weren't going to be wearing them.

Purdy was asked if he wanted to stay with the Eleventh Airborne, which he had been assigned to, and he said that he didn't. "I didn't want to make any more jumps because I was scared of it. The war was over with, and I wanted to go home." He didn't have to make any more jumps, but he didn't get to go home right away. He was assigned to the Forty-Sixth Engineer Battalion and sent to Japan, where he ran a motor pool. In April 1946, the government issued a new order saying that anyone still in the service overseas who had lost any immediate family in the war could request stateside duty. "I put in for it, and a week later, I was on my way home."

When asked if his years in the service were well spent, Purdy said, "Sort of. It was an experience that I wouldn't want to go through again, but it was a good experience. There were times when I wished I was home, of course....But I don't have bad feelings about it. I'm not sorry I went. I guess if I had it to do over again, I probably would do it again at that age."

***

ROBERT PURDY RETURNED TO Bennington and bought a house on Burgess Road. He spent most of his life as a carpenter but was also a skilled woodworker who made furniture and clocks for family and friends. He was an avid fisherman, and for a time, he held the record for the largest chain pickerel ever caught in Vermont. Despite his father having been killed in a motorcycle accident, he had a motorcycle of his own and enjoyed riding it.

Purdy and his wife, the former Jean Knights, had five children. She died in 1976, and in 1980, he married Jean Lucier, who died in 2000. Purdy himself died at the Vermont Veterans' Home on September 12, 2012. September 12 was the same day that his brother Ken had been killed by the Japanese in the Solomon Islands sixty-nine years earlier, back in 1943.

9

CARLETON CARPENTER

Probably the best known of all the Bennington people who served in the war was Carleton Upham Carpenter Jr., who entered service as a six-foot-three-inches-tall, rail-thin teenage sailor who later went on to star in many Hollywood films and Broadway plays and who had a top-selling record hit in 1950, singing "Aba Daba Honeymoon" with Debbie Reynolds in the film *Two Weeks With Love*. It was a memorable song from a forgettable movie. Carpenter had tried to join the navy while still in high school, when he was just seventeen, but had been rejected twice because of a rapid heartbeat. Right after his graduation from high school, he tried again, this time with a pill from his doctor to slow down his heartbeat. After taking more pills than he was supposed to and ending up with almost no heartbeat at all, he was nonetheless accepted, along with two others from the area who would become his close friends—Bernard Galipeau from Bennington and Dean Houghton from Arlington—and they were sent off to boot camp in Upstate New York.

Carpenter, at the time, was handsome and blond. He had been voted "best dancer" by his high school class, where he was an indifferent basketball player who spent more time on the bench than on the court, but he was a good skier and an accomplished actor and musician who played piano, violin, cello, saxophone and drums. By the end of 1943, he had all the academic credits he needed to graduate with the class of 1944, so went to Rutland during the school's holiday break to try to enlist in the navy. He had a letter from his parents giving him permission to join since he was under

Dalles, Oregon.
NEXT PAGE, COLUMN ONE

BANNER — JANUARY 29, 1945.

THREE SEABEE PALS

Left to right, Carleton Carpenter and Bernard Galipeau of Bennington, and Dean Houghton of Arlington, all seamen 2c, who entered the armed forces together last July and who have been side

This image of Carlton Carpenter and two Seabees friends originally appeared in the *Bennington Banner. Courtesy of the* Bennington Banner.

the age of eighteen at the time. When he was rejected, he took the train to Manhattan and went looking for a show to act in. He was hired on his very first day. "It was called *Bright Boy*," he later recalled. "David Merrick was the associate producer. It was his first show. The role was for a tall, lanky blond boy who was seventeen. That's what I was. I signed a contract for $57.50 a week. It was a flop."

Carpenter went back to Bennington just long enough to graduate from high school in June 1944 and then went into the navy. "Boot camp was lots of running and exercise," he recalled in an interview in 2013.

After boot camp, they put us on the oldest train I'd ever seen for a trip to Oakland that took forever. All the way across country, we kept singing "Time Waits for No One." That was from the Ann Sheridan movie Shine on Harvest Moon. It went:

It passes you by,
It rolls on forever,
Like clouds in the sky…
So, don't let us throw
One sweet moment away.
Time waits for no one.
Let's make love while we may.

It was a love song. We were just kids, but kids sang love songs back then. We sang it over and over without any feeling that it was mawkish or unmanly….Two other songs from the war years that I liked were "Tico Tico" and "Don't Fence Me In." My mother sent me the sheet music to them so I could play them. "Don't Fence Me In" was written by Cole Porter. That surprised a lot of people because it was such an un–Cole Porter sort of song.

*When we got to Oakland, they lined us up in formation and said, "Men, you are now Seabees." We said, "What the ** are seabees?" We'd never heard of seabees.*

The seabees were navy construction battalions, and the term *seabees* came from the letters C and B that were shorthand for construction battalion. They used heavy equipment to build bases as well as docks, road and airstrips. "I'd never done any construction work. None of us had," Carpenter later recalled.

But we were assigned to the Thirty-Eighth Naval Construction Battalion, which originally had been stationed in Kodiak, Alaska, and put on a troop ship for Hawaii. We were in Hawaii for two days, and one of those nights, we watched a movie from about a mile away in which Lynn Bari sang "I'm Making Believe." The three of us—me, Galipeau and Houghton—were all lined up with our cans of beer, and we sang along with her. Then we left for Tinian Island, in the Marianas, which was our final stop. When we unloaded, we were going down a cargo net, and I caught my foot and went ass over teakettle. I lost my wallet with my navy ID and sixty dollars in it.

The Americans had seized Tinian Island in August 1944, and of the 8,500-man Japanese garrison, only 313 survived. Some continued hiding and refusing to surrender, and in fact, Muratau Susumu, the last holdout on Tinian, wasn't captured until 1953. By the time Carpenter's unit arrived, there was still some shelling from Japanese artillery, but the Japanese weren't much of a threat because there weren't many of them left, and they didn't have much ammunition. "We did have our own Captain Queeg, though," Carpenter recalled, in reference to the central figure of *The Caine Mutiny*. "He didn't ask who was eating his strawberries, but he had a xylophone, and he walked around camp at night playing it. People thought that was pretty strange."

Carpenter said there were three groups of people in the seabees. There were the boots like himself who were just seventeen and eighteen years old and "didn't know what they were doing," and the "old salts" who had been in Alaska and had learned some basic construction skills. And there were the men who were forty years old and older who had worked in construction in their civilian lives and who, Carpenter said, "were the ones who knew what they were doing." One other man from Bennington in the seabees in the South Pacific was James H. Cook, a middle-aged machinist mate, first class, who, at the time, had three sons in the service, one of whom would be killed in the South Pacific while serving in the army infantry. After it was captured by the marines, fifteen thousand Seabees turned Tinian Island into the busiest airfield of the war, with six 7,900-foot runways for attacks by B-29 Bombers on enemy targets in the Philippines, the Ryukyu Islands and mainland Japan, including the firebombing of Tokyo and the atomic bombings of Hiroshima and Nagasaki. Tinian was the home base for the *Enola Gay*, the Boeing B-29 Superfortress bomber named for Enola Gay Tibbets, the mother of Colonel Paul Tibbets, who piloted the plane when it dropped the atom bomb on Hiroshima.

Carpenter didn't do much work on the runways, having been removed from construction crews after just two days with a jackhammer. Instead, he was assigned to the disbursing office, where he paid the 1,100 men in his unit every month and was in charge of the beer line. "I was supposed to make sure that no one had more than two cans of beer a night. But we also had something called 'coral cocktails' that I think were made from grapefruit juice and Vitalis hair tonic. It was pretty awful, but whatever it was, it didn't kill us."

"We lived four to a tent," Carpenter said. "We had a not-too-bad mess hall with a cook who was inventive with Spam. We had one free day a week. And night after night, we watched the bombing of Saipan, which was like fireworks." Saipan was where his fellow Bennington native Bill Kearns had been given a Bronze Star for refusing to give up his radio post after being wounded in battle. "I had a portable organ that was made by the Estey Organ Company in Brattleboro. Every Sunday, I'd lug it around and play it at four different church services. I played what church music I could remember—or at least things that sounded like church music. I didn't do any entertaining, but I did play the organ on Sundays."

Carpenter left Tinian before the war ended.

At one point, they had given all of us a test and picked people who had scored in the top four for officer's candidate school. I had come in third. I didn't want to go because Galipeau and Houghton and I had become very tight. So, I left with a heavy heart. They put me on a small plane—it was the first time I'd ever been on a plane—and flew me to Saipan. I looked down on the strip where my friends were working, and I got all teared up. It happened so fast that I never even got to say goodbye. They put me on a bigger plane to Hawaii, and I landed the day that FDR died. Then they put me on a ship to San Francisco, and from there, I went to New York. I was supposed to go to Princeton for the officer's candidate school training, but my second day in New York, my appendix burst, and I ended up in the Brooklyn Naval Hospital.

He never went back to active duty.

***

BERNARD GALIPEAU RETURNED TO Bennington and lived to be eighty-four years old. He raised a family of five children, worked as a pressman at the BenMont Paper Company and was a founder of the local chapter of Disabled American Veterans. He spent much of his time hunting and fishing. Dean Houghton became a highly successful Vermont high school basketball and football coach, and then, he became a high school principal and was elected to the Vermont Principals' Association High School Sports Hall of Fame. Carpenter went on to have a long and successful career in films, television and on Broadway, and he took part in a long-running tour with the national company of *Hello, Dolly!* that included appearances before the troops in Vietnam. He also appeared in *Crazy for You* and *The Boys in the Band*. He returned to Bennington often to take part in plays staged by Oldcastle Theatre, a local Actors' Equity company, appearing there for the last time when he was ninety years old.

10

HELEN RUDD BEARDON

Helen Rudd was born in East Arlington in 1922, and aside from attending nursing school in Pittsfield and her time in the service, she lived in Arlington her entire life. She had two younger brothers in the service—one a navigator/bombardier in the army air corps and one in the navy. Both joined late in the war, and neither left the United States; neither did Helen, whose poor eyesight prohibited her from overseas duty.

Helen was in nurse's training when Pearl Harbor was bombed. She finished her training, joined the army nurse corps in March 1945 and did her basic training at Fort Devens in Ayer, Massachusetts. It was while shopping in an Ayer department store that she heard the news on the radio that President Roosevelt had died. She was first posted to Camp Edwards on Cape Cod, which was treating many who had been injured in the European theater. One of her patients was Oscar Linke, who she had gone to high school with in Arlington. Linke, whose father had made picture frames for Norman Rockwell when he was living and painting his *Saturday Evening Post* covers in Arlington, had enlisted in the army in 1944. Because he spoke German, he had been used as an interpreter. He was wounded twice and ended up in a German hospital before being moved to Cape Cod. Another Arlington native who she knew, Staff Sergeant John Henry Forkey, was wounded three times while fighting in Africa, Sicily and Italy, and then he was killed in the Battle of the Bulge.

Rudd was transferred from the army to the army air corps and sent to an airbase at Santa Ana, California. Most of the patients there were prisoners of war who were treated mainly by corpsmen with the nurses supervising them. There were some Japanese and Italian patients, but most of them were German. "Some could speak English, but I can remember them getting very upset at us at times when we couldn't understand what they were trying to tell us," she recalled. "But generally, they were good to take care of. They were young fellows that probably were homesick and didn't know what was going to happen to them in this country."

> Interviewer. *So, you felt some sympathy toward them?*
> Rudd. *Somewhat, yes. Our feeling was they weren't to blame. They had to fight. I think all of the girls understood their situation, so we were kind to them and did what we had to. It was a strange situation. We were in locked wards with military police coming through.*

One of the patients she treated, Robert Whitman, was so appreciative that he later had a plaque placed in her honor at the Women's Military Memorial in Washington, D.C.

Rudd was still at Santa Ana on V-J Day and stayed there through Christmas 1945. And some of these were good times—even fun times—for her.

> *They had nurses go with the patients to football games and shows in the Los Angeles area. We went to the Stage Door Canteen and the Friar's Club. That was always a lot of fun. My brother was in town on Christmas morning, and we went to the "Breakfast Club" show that used to be on the radio. They went around asking some of us where we were from. They asked my name and hometown. So, everyone* [back in Arlington] *was calling mother and dad because they heard me. They gave us a folder with a five-dollar bill in it. At that time, it seemed like a lot. Then we went to a place where there were foreign pilots in training, and there was a party going on. Someone invited all of us up to Lauren Bacall's for dinner on Christmas Day. So, we went up there in the hills, where she had a beautiful view. We had dinner there. She was really very nice.*

Rudd—who, by then, was married to Hal Beardon, an air corps pilot who she flew with often on his training flights, and pregnant with her son, John—was discharged in May 1947. She and her husband were stationed in San Antonio. He was transferred to Louisiana, and she decided to divorce him and move back to Arlington.

Helen Rudd Beardon.
Courtesy of her son.

Helen Rudd Beardon was only one of the many Bennington County women to serve in the war. Marie Tetreault served with the army nursing corps in Hawaii. J. Elisabetta Cartwright of Bennington and Virginia Dare Keene of North Bennington became ensigns in the WAVES. Pharmacist mate, second class, Elsie Balmer of North Bennington worked with convalescing patients at the navy hospital in Santa Cruz. Lillian Docherty went from being a machine operator at the E.Z. Mills to serving in naval hospitals in Bethesda, Maryland, and Corpus Christi, Texas. Florence Patterson joined the WAVES, as did Rachel Stratton, Phyllis Payne, Elsie Williams and Iona Lemieux. Ida Livingston joined the SPARS, which was the women's coast guard. Hazel Baker joined the U.S. Women's Army Corps, or WACS, as did Beatrice Breese, Ann Barker, Hazel Baker Ojsack, Nancy Dennis, Nora Buck, Florence Miller, Elizabeth Healy, Mary Jewett, Arlene and Pauline Sanborn, Elizabeth Peabody and Helen Carhart, among others. Patricia Ryan, who had been a star athlete at Bennington High School, served in a WACS headquarters company in Naples and played on her company's softball team in the shadow of Mount Vesuvius.

***

AFTER THE WAR, HELEN Rudd Beardon lived with her parents for a time on their Arlington farm. She then taught nurses at Putnam Memorial Hospital and eventually became the industrial nurse at the local Union Carbine plant. She was a Daughter of the American Revolution and a lifetime member of American Legion Post 69 of Arlington. She died of cancer on April 20, 2004.

11

GERALD MORRISSEY

Gerald Morrissey was living in South Hamilton, Massachusetts, when the war broke out. Hamilton was originally called "Hamlet" when it was founded in 1638, but it was then named for Alexander Hamilton in 1793. It was the home of General George Patton and was a place of historic houses, stone walls and an equestrian heritage that Morrissey was not a part of since he owned no horses and wasn't a fox hunter or a polo player—both of which were major pastimes in Hamilton. He and his wife, Phyllis, had driven to Gloucester and then to Essex earlier that day to tour those charming harbor villages and had bought a peck of clams for ninety-eight cents. They were driving back home with the clams when they heard about the bombing of Pearl Harbor on the car radio.

Morrissey had been born in Bennington on December 12, 1916. There were three boys and six girls in the family, and he was the next-to-youngest child. He grew up on Washington Avenue and walked back and forth to the Bennington Grade School and then to the high school, each of them about a half mile away. Like most children in Bennington at the time, he'd walk home for lunch and then walk back to school for afternoon classes. He was a "*Banner* Boy" who delivered the afternoon *Bennington Banner* newspaper, which paid him two cents a week for each customer. The owner of the *Bennington Banner*, Frank Howe, also was the postmaster, and through him, Morrissey got a second daily job delivering "special delivery" mail on a bicycle. He made about fifteen dollars a week from that, which was much more than he made from his paper route.

Gerald Morrissey. *Courtesy of his daughter, Mary Morrissey.*

Morrissey played guard on his high school football team, where the fullback was Louis Perrotta, who would go on to play football at Ithaca and then serve five years in the army during World War II, most of it in the South Pacific. One of the halfbacks was John Maloney, who later served in the army in Africa and Europe. One of the ends was "Red" Hurley, who served as a seabee in the South Pacific. And the quarterback was Nick Marra, an accomplished saxophone and piano player who attended Norwich University and won a Bronze Star for heroism as an army captain in the Pacific. Marra's sister Geraldine married Robert Sausville, who flew his B-24 Liberation bomber on fifty-eight missions in the Pacific. That 1933 team was undefeated until the last game of the season, when, while playing Fair Haven and leading 6–0, with almost no time left, Marra fumbled a Fair Haven punt on his own nine-yard line. Fair Haven recovered and scored to win, 7–6, which was of no great import but was something that Morrissey, nonetheless, grumbled about for the rest of his very long life. "We never forgave him," he was still saying about Marra nearly seventy years later.

Morrissey went to college at Notre Dame, where he played football on the practice squad that the varsity scrimmaged against and had a bit part on the movie *Knute Rockne, All American* that was filmed on the campus during his senior year. After graduating with an engineering degree, he went to work for the New England Power Association, designing lighting systems for businesses in the Salem and Gloucester area. He then went to Sault Saint Marie, Michigan, where he worked on the MacArthur Lock, which was built to allow ships to travel between Lake Superior and the Lower Great Lakes. Just as that job was being completed, in July 1943, the navy recruited twenty-one of the engineers from that project to join the seabees, which Morrissey decided to do rather than be drafted into the army. His recruitment also meant that he'd enter the service as an officer—first as an ensign and later as a lieutenant, junior grade—rather than as an enlisted man. His wife went back to South Bend, where she had grown up and where her parents were still living, while Morrissey went, first, to basic training at Camp Perry in Virginia and then to Camp Endicott in Rhode Island.

During a short leave after training at Camp Endicott, Morrissey went back to Bennington, went deer hunting with friends and shot a 150-pound buck that he had carved up at Shanahan's Grocery and Meat Market and gave away the venison to his brother, Francis; the man who had loaned him the rifle to go hunting with; and several friends. He then went to the New York City waterfront for a month to learn how to oversee stevedores loading ships and then to a chemical warfare school outside Baltimore, Maryland.

Before shipping out for the Pacific, Morrissey worked out a code with his wife that he could use in letters he wrote her that would let her know just where he was, which was information usually cut out of letters by military censors. He first went to Hawaii, where he spent close to six months in the Pearl Harbor area and met up with another person from Bennington, Second Lieutenant Marie Tetreault, who was in the army nursing corps there. He then went to Iwo Jima, where his unit arrived twenty-eight days after the marines had first landed. Iwo Jima was one of the bloodiest battles of the war in the Pacific, but most of the fighting was over with by the time Morrissey's unit arrived. "We went aground on landing craft with packs on our backs, so we were a part of the invasion force, even though it was late in the fighting," he recalled many years later. "We didn't see any combat, but there were still Japs on the north end of the island." But while they didn't see any combat, Morrissey lost ten seabees friends when a truck they were riding in drove over a mine that the Japanese had buried in the middle of a road.

The seabees built airfields and Quonset huts on Iwo Jima, and Morrissey was in charge of building several of the forty-by-one-hundred-foot Quonset huts. Two of the airfields were long ones for B-29 bombers, and the third was a shorter one for fighter planes.

At the time the atom bomb was dropped on Hiroshima, Morrissey's unit had all of its equipment loaded onto a ship and was preparing for the invasion of Japan. When asked in the spring of 2000 if he thought the decision to drop the bomb was the right one, Morrissey said, "Absolutely. If not, we'd have been a goner. Our seabee battalion would have gone into the Tokyo Bay area attached to a marine division. God knows what might have happened there."

Morrissey spent two and a half months in Japan after the war ended, and then he had enough points for a discharge and his return home. He arranged for a place on a battleship that was headed for Seattle, but several days into the trip, the battleship got orders to head for Pearl Harbor instead. He was then transferred to an old aircraft carrier that was headed to San Francisco. "When we went through the swells leading into San Francisco

Bay, boy did I get seasick," he said. "I was seasick for two days." But he then caught a train to Chicago, where his wife met him at the train station. They first went back to South Bend and then to Bennington, where they lived for the rest of their lives.

***

GERALD AND PHYLLIS MORRISSEY raised a family of four sons and two daughters, one of whom—Mary Morrissey—became a long-time member of the Vermont state legislature. Morrissey himself became a general contractor, and the first building he constructed was a Knights of Columbus hall on Main Street that now is the Bennington Performing Arts Center Theater. Morrissey was a long-time member of the Knights of Columbus, along with the Elks Club, the American Legion, the Hale Mountain Rod & Gun Club and the Rattlesnake Club. He enjoyed hunting, fishing and golfing and was a trustee of Bennington Catholic High School. He died in 2002, just a few days before his eighty-sixth birthday.

12

LEROY "LARRY" DUNN

eroy Dunn, who preferred to be called Larry, was born in Bennington on January 30, 1925. Until he was fifteen, his family lived in South Shaftsbury, where one of his first jobs, at the age of eleven, was taking care of pheasants for the local Fish and Game Club. On the day after the attack on Pearl Harbor, he and his parents went across the road to his grandfather's house, where they turned on the large and ornate Atwater Kent radio in the parlor and heard President Roosevelt say, "We are at war."

Shortly after that, the family moved to Manchester, and Dunn switched from North Bennington High School to Burr & Burton Academy. He graduated in 1943, when he was eighteen, and he immediately went to Rutland and tried to enlist in the navy. He was rejected because of poor eyesight. He then went to a recruiter in Bennington, who said if the only physical problem was his eyesight, he could still join the seabees. "Sure. Why not?" Dunn said, and he enlisted.

He trained at Camp Perry, Virginia, near Williamsburg, where the boot camp drill instructors were marines. He was then sent to Camp Endicott, Rhode Island, for advanced training and then to Pearl Harbor on the USS *Harris*, wearing heavy winter clothing that was more suited to Alaska than Hawaii. He and his company spent most of their time making Quonset huts that were shipped to islands in the South Pacific that marines had captured and were establishing permanent bases at, including Midway, Guam, New Hebrides, Iwo Jima and Saipan. At one point while he was on

Hawaii, he was tracked down by Gerald Morrissey, who had spotted on list somewhere that a seabee from Bennington was stationed there. "I know your folks," Morrissey told him.

Dunn spent the war in Pearl Harbor, living in a Quonset hut he had helped build and operating heavy equipment and cranes while making fifty-five dollars a month. The men were allowed to go swimming at Waikiki Beach, but Dunn only did it once because the coral cut his feet. "We were so overjoyed when the war ended!" he recalled in an interview in 2000. "We went down to our base in Iroquois Point. We celebrated there for a day and a half. Whistles were blowing, and barges were pumping water in the air, and all kinds of flags were flying, and there was a lot of kissing and hugging going on!"

He said he was "100 percent behind the decision" to drop the bombs on Hiroshima and Nagasaki. He saw the damage done on newsreel films by Lowell Thomas and couldn't believe the damage done by a single bomb. He never came under any fire during the war, and the only casualties he saw were in May 1944, when an explosion in a staging area for ships being loaded with ammunition and fuel and other supplies for the Second and Fourth Marine Divisions caused a huge fireball that resulted in at least 169 dead and 396 wounded. Dunn was pulled off his crane and ordered to get on an ambulance and help bring back the casualties. "Boy, it was pathetic to see some of those fellows, the way they were wounded," he said. "Oh, God, it was awful."

At one point, Dunn and a seabee friend volunteered for combat, asking to be allowed to join the marines in the invasion of Iwo Jima. An officer refused their request, telling them, "I'm sorry, but you can't do that. It's very commendable that you want to, but I need your services right here as much as they probably need you over there." After hearing about the huge number of casualties inflicted on the marines on Iwo Jima, Dunn and his friend told one another that they might have been too gung-ho in volunteering and that the officer had done them a big favor in rejecting them.

"I thought I was pretty fortunate during the war years to have done what I did but still not have to go to combat," he said.

***

DUNN CAME BACK TO Bennington and first took a job in Rutland at the Howe Scale Company, then in Bennington at the EZ Mill and, later, Union

Carbide. He met his wife, Pauline "Polly" Kittel at the EZ Mill, where she was working as a sewing machine operator along with her mother and sister. They had a son and a daughter, and he spent much of his time hunting, raising beagles, operating a sugar shack and riding his motorcycle and snowmobile. He died in 2009 at the age of eighty-four, one year after his wife.

13

NORMAN F. MYERS

Private first class Norman F. Myers, who was a company clerk with Company A, Fifty-Second Armored Infantry Regiment, Ninth Armored Division, was captured along with most of his unit on December 17, 1944, after being overrun by the Germans during the Battle of the Bulge. He was declared "missing in action" on December 18, and it wasn't until February 22, 1945, that his parents in Bennington got a letter from him saying that he was a prisoner of war in Germany. He remained a prisoner until May 7, 1945, when the Germans closed down the camp near Zittau while trying to avoid the Russians who were about to liberate it. Zittau was in the most northeastern part of Germany, near the borders of both Poland and Czechoslovakia, and most of the Americans found their way into Czechoslovakia and back into American hands. Myers rejoined the American forces on May 12. He was twenty-three-years-old and had lost half his body weight while in prison.

Norman Francis Myers, first known as "Sonny" and later as "Norm," was born on January 30, 1922, to John Joseph Myers (whose name had originally been Maillard) and Jennie Ella Stratton. He was the oldest of what would be five children. John Myers was a mill worker, and Jennie was descended from Joel Stratton, who had been a Revolutionary War soldier in Colonel Samuel Herrick's "Green Mountain Rangers" militia that had fought at the Battle of Bennington. Although he didn't know it when he was alive, a daughter later had a genealogy compiled by an expert of the Middle Ages who said that he was descended on his father's side from Charlemagne, all of the Plantagenet

Norman "Sonny" Myers was captured at the Battle of the Bulge and was a prisoner of war in Zittau, Germany. *Provided to Find A Grave by his family.*

kings and many other British notables. But at the time of his birth, Myers was directly descended from an unremarkable mill worker at the Ben-Mont Paper Mill.

The family's small home with no telephone was located at 316 Safford Street in Bennington, which was a short walk away from Bennington High School, where Myers—large for his age—played football and basketball. He was captain of the 1939–40 basketball team, which started slow but improved as the season went along, developing into one of the best teams the high school had ever had, losing the state championship to heavily favored Cathedral High School of Burlington by a single point. Myers, who was six feet, three inches tall and wore number 35, was, according to the *Bennington Banner* when he came home from the war, "one of Ben-Hi's star basketball players."

It's not known where Myers worked between his graduation in 1940 and induction into the army in 1942, but a daughter believes that he may have driven a truck. His military record says that his civilian occupation had been "shipping clerk." His registration for the draft report on June 30, 1942, said that he was six feet, three inches tall, weighed 185 pounds and had blue eyes, brown hair and a light complexion.

Myers was inducted on November 13, 1942, and went on active duty on November 27 at Fort Devens, Massachusetts. By December, he was with the Fifty-Second Armored Infantry Regiment at Fort Riley, Kansas, where he spent eight weeks in a hospital after injuring his left knee while playing football for the regimental team. Later, while on desert maneuvers in California, he was injured again when a half-track vehicle he was riding in had a door blown in by a land mine that went off when it shouldn't have. He spent time in Farney General Hospital in Palm Springs, California, and then, in January 1944, he rejoined his unit at Camp Polk, Louisiana, where he was a company clerk in the battalion headquarters.

Myers left the United States on August 20, 1944, sailing with his unit on the *Queen Mary* and docking on August 26 in the Firth of Clyde on the west coast of Scotland. He was stationed in England for six weeks, and then his unit was sent to Cherbourg, France, and, later, into Luxembourg. While in Luxembourg, he drove a "peep" called *Ace of Diamonds* for the executive officer—a "peep" being what the armored units called their Jeeps. That allowed him to see a good deal of Luxembourg.

The Ninth Armored Division that he was a part of was called the "Phantom Division." That was because, in the weeks before D-Day, it was camped on the British coastline opposite of the German defenses at Pas-de-Calais, trying to deceive the Germans into thinking that's where the invasion would take place. So, it was a phantom division that was never intended to take part in the invasion. At the time of the Battle of the Bulge, it had seen almost no action, but it was later cited for extraordinary heroism and gallantry after its units—outnumbered five to one, totally surrounded by the enemy and with clerks, cooks, drivers and mechanics being pressed into combat—beat back repeated German attacks over a six-day period and allowed other American units to fight their way into the Ardennes and defeat the German offensive.

Myers's unit was ordered into battle on December 16, and he and most of his company were taken prisoner on December 17. They were marched across Germany for more than two weeks and then were transported farther east by rail or truck convoys. It was a painful trip, with little food, medical treatment or warm clothing. As one of the prisoners wrote after returning home in the summer of 1945:

> *My feet were badly frostbitten, as well as three of my fingers. We did get a small amount of bread every other day, with a little cheese, as well as a small amount of water and some weak coffee. We also got one Red Cross box for ten men on the last day. Then we were loaded on boxcars (60 men to a car) with no straw or heat in them, and at night, we didn't have room to lie down but were forced to stand or sit. There were no latrines; the only means of relieving ourselves were by cans or boxes or in the car itself. Many of the fellows had bad cases of dysentery, and conditions were terrible. We spent a total of four days in the box car. One day, we had a small amount of soup. The rest of the time, we did without water or food. They kept the door locked at all times to prevent escape. Finally, we were let out and marched about three miles to a small woods through snow that was quite deep. The temperature at this time was below zero, and we were forced to stand in this grove of woods for nearly four hours. Finally, we were taken in smaller groups into the camp itself. We later learned that we were at Camp*

IV-B, near Leipzig or Muhlburg. This ended the first phase of our being prisoners of war. Up to this time, we were "missing in action" only and were not technically prisoners.

It was January 7, 1945, when the prisoners from the 9th Armored Division arrived, having been in transit for more than three weeks. Stalag IV-B was one of the largest prisoner of war camps in Germany. Stalag is an abbreviation of the German *stammlager*, which means "main camp," and Stalag IV-B was located just east of the Elbe River, about thirty miles north of Dresden. The first prisoners there were seventeen thousand Polish soldiers captured in 1939. French prisoners were added in 1940; British prisoners captured in North Africa were added in 1941; and then many Russians came from the invasion of Russia. Eventually, Americans were added to the camp, including the novelist Kurt Vonnegut, an infantry scout who also had been captured at the Battle of the Bulge when his 106th Infantry Division was totally overrun, with five hundred killed and six thousand captured.

In February 1945, Myers and about three hundred other lower-ranking Americans, none of them officers, were transferred to Abbeits Kommando 1315, a few miles northeast of Zittau. There, they basically did road and rail construction with picks and shovels, getting up at 5:00 a.m. and returning at 6:00 p.m., but they were usually allowed to stop work at 3:00 p.m. on Sundays. Church services were held on Sunday evenings, but very few—seldom more than two dozen—attended. They lived in three barracks that had small stoves that kept them reasonably warm, but food was an endless problem. Breakfast was plain flour and water, and dinner was a small piece of bread and a watery soup with potatoes. About once a week, there would be meat but generally no more than a tablespoon of it. On rare occasions, they got Red Cross boxes that they considered wonderful because they contained cans of sardines, salmon, corned beef and Spam, along with cheese and sugar and raisins or prunes and a chocolate bar. But one of the three barracks only got two boxes while they were there. The result of the heavy work and minimal food was malnutrition and starvation. Of the 300 Americans who arrived in February, only 111 remained by Easter. Eleven had died, three had been shot trying to escape and the rest were in sick barracks. Body lice were another big problem.

Finally, on May 5, they were told that the war was ending, that the camp was being closed and that they would be marched into Czechoslovakia and turned over to the Americans rather than the Russians.

Myers arrived back in the United States on June 12, 1945, and was discharged from Fort Devens on December 16. He had a total foreign service time of nine months and twenty-three days, more than half of it as a POW. According to his discharge papers, his weight was back up to 215 pounds at the time. They said he had qualified as an expert with a rifle and as a marksman with a carbine and that his military specialty was as a "rifleman." They said that he had been awarded an American Theater Campaign Ribbon, a Victory Medal and a Good Conduct Medal. He was given a mustering out pay of $300.

***

MYERS MARRIED MARGARET TREMBLY on April 6, 1947, and they had five daughters. He became a carpenter and lived first in Hoosick Falls, New York, and then Wappingers Falls, where his last job was as the maintenance carpenter at Marist College in Poughkeepsie. While in Hoosick, he was elected exalter rule of the Elks Lodge, and he enjoyed flying planes at the Rhinebeck Aerodrome. He was sixty-two years old when he died in 1964.

14

JOSEPH KRAWCZYK

oseph Krawczyk was born on February 22, 1919, which, back then, was celebrated as George Washington's birthday. His parents had come from Poland, which made them rarities in Bennington, where most of the immigrants were either Irish or French-Canadian, with a scattering of Greek and Lebanese immigrants who owned some of the most popular grocery stores and restaurants. His father was a mill worker, and his mother was a housewife with thirteen children, of which he was the twelfth.

Krawczyk joined the national guard right out of high school. "I could see the war coming," he later said. "And I figured if I joined the guard, if we did go, we'd go as a group, and we'd go with people we knew. That's the main reason I didn't want to be a draftee. The reason I joined was to be with Bennington boys, and we pretty much stayed together during the war. Some of us were transferred out to different units, but I stayed with the Vermont unit all the way through."

The Vermonters were a part of the 43rd Infantry Division, which included troops from Connecticut, Maine, Vermont and Rhode Island. The Vermont unit was the 172nd Infantry Regiment. Eventually, the 43rd became known at the "Winged Victory Division" after Major General Leonard F. Wing of Rutland became its commander in August 1943.

The Bennington unit was inducted on February 24, 1941. It trained first at Camp Blanding, Florida, where Krawczyk was transferred from Bennington's Company I to Company A, which was from Brattleboro. Company A was an antitank unit, and he stayed with it until the end of the war. The Forty-Third then went to Camp Shelby, Mississippi, then to Fort Ord, California, and

Captain Joseph Krawczyk Sr. is shown in a tinted studio portrait wearing a green army dress uniform. *Courtesy of the Bennington Museum.*

then to the Solomon Islands. Eventually, it went island hopping from one island to another—New Caledonia, Guadalcanal and New Guinea. "From 1942 until 1945, I was in the jungles," Krawczyk said. "I had a short break. In 1943, we went to New Zealand for about six weeks. Then it was back to New Guinea."

The Forty-Third Division ran into problems from the start, when the ship taking it to the fighting, the SS *President Coolidge*, struck two mines in New Hebrides Harbor and capsized. Before the war, the *President Coolidge* had been a luxury ocean liner that had room for 1,260 passengers (350 of them in first class) and a crew of 300. It had been launched in 1931, when Grace Coolidge, the former president's wife, had christened it with a bottle of water from a brook on the Coolidge family farm in Plymouth, Vermont. Only two lives were lost, but a great deal of equipment was lost, along with the entire stock of quinine held by the military at the time. The mines, in fact, were American mines, but no one had told the captain of the *President Coolidge* that the entrance to the harbor had been mined, and he was acquitted in the court-martial that followed.

"We hit two mines," Krawczyk recalled in an interview with the Bennington Historical Society.

The ship just bounced right up in the air and back again. After the first mine hit, I grabbed my life jacket and tightened it down. The ship came to a screeching halt. It stood right there and began listing to one side—you could see it tipping. They gave us orders to abandon ship and to leave all the gear on the ship—weapons, clothing, just go overboard with what you had on.

Krawczyk swam from the ship to the island and ended up covered with oil from the ship's ruptured fuel tanks. The expectation was that the ship would remain upright and that much of the food, clothing, weapons and equipment could be unloaded later. But soon after the more than 5,300 men made it to shore, the ship blew up and sank.

Lieutenant Colonel John "Tipper" Carrigan was killed by Japanese artillery during the battle of Luzon. *Courtesy of the* Bennington Banner.

It was two months before the Forty-Third was reequipped with clothing, equipment and weapons, and it then left for Guadalcanal, which had been pretty much secured by marines by the time it got there. From there, it went to Rendova, where it landed on July 1, 1943. Krawczyk was a lieutenant by then, having been given a battlefield commission, and the Vermont infantry was being commanded by Major John F. Carrigan of Bennington, who was known as "Tipper."

Right after Guadalcanal, Krawczyk's unit was fighting on Arundel, a small island in the Solomons, and it had a carrying party coming up a trail through the jungle, bringing food and supplies. "The Japanese were on one side of the trail, and we were on the other side, just a matter of a few yards—forty or fifty yards—shooting at each other," he recalled.

Here comes this carrying party, and who was in it but Kenneth Purdy from Bennington. We tried to stop the carrying party. We put our hands down on the ground shouting, "Hold it, hold it." They didn't see us. They kept on coming between us and the Japanese. And they got him—the Japs got him. They killed Ken Purdy and several others....I came back from that battle with ten or twelve men out of thirty men. So, that was a rough one. At that time, I was in charge of a platoon. So, imagine going in with a bunch of them and coming back with a handful.

The Vermonters lost their commander on Rosario in the Philippines. "Tipper" Carrigan, who most in Bennington thought had a promising future in the law and in politics, had been promoted to colonel. He was also a newlywed, having met and married a New Zealand woman during the unit's brief stop there. He was killed when the Japanese, using horse-drawn artillery, fired a shell right into the cave in a hillside that he was using as his command post. Krawczyk helped dig his body out of the rubble.

Interviewer. *What was the worst thing about living in the jungle?*
Krawczyk. *Well, it's hard to explain. You live like an animal. I remember, one time, we were on Guadalcanal. It was hot, and we were hot and dirty.*

We found a stream but couldn't take a bath because the mosquitos were so thick. The minute you took your shirt off, you were covered with mosquitos. So, we had to give orders to put shirts back on because we had to fight malarias over there.

I picked it up over there. However, I was one of the lucky ones. I took my medicine. They gave us medicine every day. A lot of the boys would throw it away, but I took mine. However, when I got home in 1945, it was in my system. I got home and said to myself, "Well, we're home—I don't have to take that medicine any more." About a month later, I came down with malaria and almost died.

Krawczyk was wounded twice and was cited for gallantry in action at Ipo Dam, where he risked his life to move a wounded soldier from an exposed position to safety, despite having himself been wounded by grenade fragments just moments before. In all, he was awarded a Silver Star for Gallantry in Action, a Bronze Star for Valor and two Purple Hearts.

The Forty-Third Division was still in the Philippines, preparing to invade Japan when the war ended. It had suffered 1,128 killed in action, 4,887 wounded in action, had 9 missing in action and 2 taken prisoner. Krawczyk always felt there would have been many more if the atom bomb hadn't been dropped. "It saved my life," he said. "And it saved the lives of a lot of boys. It's a hell of a thing to say for them people over there, but we probably would have lost thousands, thousands of boys getting in there. I know it was a tough decision, but when people ask me, I say, 'Well, that's the reason I'm here today.'"

***

AFTER THE WAR, KRAWCZYK went to work at Union Carbine and helped reorganize the national guard in Bennington. His unit was called into active duty during the Korean War and was sent to Germany. He ended up spending twenty-three years in active or reserve duty and retired as a lieutenant colonel. He and his wife had eight children, and he died in January 2013 at the age of ninety-three.

CONCLUSION

Vermont sent about 50,000 people into the service during World War II, nearly 1,400 of them women. In all, 1,233 Vermonters died, 52 of them from Bennington County. Vermonters bought $263,500,000 in war bonds, and in the second half of 1943, the state led the nation in the per capita amount of scrap that went toward the war effort, including many discarded plows and many of the ornate Victorian cast iron fences that towns had placed around cemeteries. The plows were important because one plow was said to have enough steel to turn into one hundred seventy-five-millimeter armor-piercing shells. And in Bennington—where people collected iron, aluminum, paper and rubber—the slogan for one of the scrap drives was, "A piece of scrap for every Jap."

While there was a lot of rationing and many shortages of things, some places prospered during the war. Springfield, the home of several large machine tool plants that made parts for bombers, had large numbers of draft-deferred mechanics working long shifts and making more money than they ever had before. Farmers in Addison County benefited from the stepped-up need of the military for eggs, milk and poultry. The woolen mills in Winooski had booming business in military contracts. And in Bennington, like everywhere else, women began taking on many of the jobs that had previously been filled by men.

This attempt to tell the story of Bennington during the war was never intended to be definitive or complete. It may, in fact, be too late for that.

Staff Sergeant Anthony Pello was a paratrooper captured on D-Day. He spent the rest of the war in a prisoner of war camp. *Courtesy of the Bennington Banner.*

Most who lived through the war as adults now are dead, and very few of them left behind any oral or written accounts. There were many exploits and adventures that were noted only in a paragraph or two in the local newspaper or an occasional letter home that still survives. For example, Anthony Pello was captured after parachuting into Normandy on D-Day and spent the rest of the war in a German prisoner of war camp. But all that seems to remain in print is a small one-column picture of him in uniform, with a headline saying "In Nazi Prison" and a single paragraph saying, "Staff Sgt. Anthony J. Pello, first local paratrooper to be reported missing in action as of D-Day, is a prisoner of war." But he came home, got married and had three children. He lived to be ninety-three years old, outliving nine sisters and brothers, and was known as an avid supporter of high school athletics, not only the traditional football, basketball and baseball teams, but also boys wrestling and girls basketball.

For many years, veterans of the war seldom talked about it. My own father, for example, spent more than four years in the army, much of it with an antiaircraft battery that was sent to Hawaii to guard against the second attack on Pearl Harbor, which, of course, never came. The only war story he ever told us was: "I dug the deepest foxhole on Okinawa." That began changing in 1998, when Tom Brokaw wrote his book *The Greatest Generation*, which sparked a renewed interest in the war. And the oral histories that make up the bulk of this book were collected in 2000 by the Bennington Historical Society, in part, because of the wildly popular reception that greeted Brokaw's work. But there are fewer than two dozen of those, and for the great majority of men and women from Bennington who served, the only record that remains are very brief and sketchy accounts that appeared in the *Bennington Banner*, many of them based on press releases from the military, but many of them were also based on second- and thirdhand hearsay from letters sent home and from fragmentary accounts by servicemen and women home on leave.

The many fragments, nonetheless, give a sense of the commitments made by so many people at so many different levels and help give us a picture of a community at war. It's from material like this that we know that Sergeant Richard Bellemare, who was with the army in the Pacific, was wounded for the second time on his birthday, September 21, 1943; that Mr. and Mrs. James Maloney of Dewey Street had five sons in the service: Robert in the navy, Edward and Joseph in the air corps and John and Andrew in the army; and that Staff Sergeant Edward Knapp, a waist gunner on a B-17 who was reported as missing in action over France, was "safe and in good hands" after being rescued by the French underground and helped back to England.

We know that Robert A. Sausville, who flew fifty-eight missions on his B-24 Liberator bomber, had been promoted to captain in 1945 and was expected home soon to rejoin his wife, the former Geraldine Marra, and to see his six-month-old daughter, Sharon Elizabeth, for the first time. We know that local nurses Madeline Willis and Frances Mooney had joined the army at Fort Ethan Allen Hospital; that Ruth Hulett, an army nurse stationed in Africa, had been promoted; and that Grace Elizabeth Everett had received her wings as a U.S. Woman Air Force Service Pilot (WASP).

We know that Staff Sergeant James Pleasant was wounded in action over Germany while serving as a gunner on the bomber *Yankee Doodle Dandy*. We know that Sergeant Truman Noyes was wounded in the right shoulder in Italy; that Lieutenant Grant Pratt, who was flying with Chennault's "Flying Tigers" in China, was reported safe after first being listed as missing in action; and that Private Peter Hill, a paratrooper, was wounded in action in Holland. We know that Private Robert Roy, the former manager of the A&P Store, was awarded a Bronze Star for meritorious service with the field artillery in France. We know that Corporal Roy Hazelton—who had a brother with Patton's Third Army in Belgium and another in the navy—suffered a shoulder wound in the Pacific. We know that Gunner's Mate, Second Class, Edward Carroll took part in the D-Day invasion; that Sergeant Earl Malon was awarded the Air Medal as a turret gunner on bombing missions over Italy; and that Private Walfrid Whalquist, one of the first Bennington men to enlist, was wounded at Anzio.

We know that Mrs. Charlotte Davis of Dewey Street had five sons in the service: Technical Sergeant Eugene, who was in the Solomon Islands; Norman, who was an army medic in China; Private Donald, who survived the attack on Pearl Harbor; James, who was an aviation cadet in Georgia; and John, who was training with the field artillery at Fort Bragg. We know that Sergeant Burton H. Turner, who had played trombone with a local orchestra before the war, was seriously wounded in France and that he survived and lived to be eighty-eight years old. We know that Staff Sergeant

Philip Sallisky was awarded the Distinguished Flying Cross as a fifty-caliber waist gunner on a Flying Fortress bomber. We know that Second Lieutenant Richard Fonteneau, the pilot of a B-17 bomber, was shot down over Romania and spent time in a Romanian prison, eventually returning home to become a plumbing contractor and have seven children, but he died young, at just forty-seven years old.

We know that First Lieutenant Raymond Foulds was wounded just outside Rome and returned to the United States to recuperate at the Fort Devens Hospital. We know that Technical Sergeant Raymond Harwood, a gunner on a bomber who had shot down at least one Messerschmitt, was a prisoner in Austria. The *Bennington Banner* reprinted parts of a letter he wrote to his parents saying that he was fine, that "our grub here is really pretty good" and that, with snow on the ground, Austria reminded him of home. He spent two years as a prisoner of war after his plane was shot down, and he came home to marry, have three children and live a life that included a lot of hunting, fishing and carpentry work.

We know that Private First Class John Harwood and Private First Class Samuel Kelson Jr. served side by side as gunners on a carrier in the South Pacific and were awarded four Bronze Stars and two Silver Stars. We know that Private First Class Arthur Welch and Private First Class Edward Roberts were wounded in France. Welch later died of his wounds. We know that Lieutenant Frederick Dunn, a B-24 Liberator bomber pilot, made his way back to his base in Italy, despite leg and ankle injuries after being forced down over France. Before flying bombers, he had been better known for his secretarial skills, having graduated from St. Joseph's Business College, and he was a state champion in contests held for typing and shorthand. He stayed in the service and retired as a lieutenant colonel, with his service including more than 150 flights, bringing supplies into Berlin during the Berlin Blockade. We know that Otto Bennett III, who left Bennington with the national guard and served in the South Pacific, was promoted from first lieutenant to captain. We know that the Arlie Greene family of South Shaftsbury had three sons in the service: Raymond, a seaman in Pensacola; Private First Class Donald, who was with Patton's army in Germany; and Corporal Cecil, who landed at D-Day. We know that Sergeant John H. Schramm, a twenty-year-old gunner on a Liberator bomber, was first declared missing and then dead, and that Captain Charles "Blackie" White, a West Point graduate from North Bennington who had been captured at Corregidor, was killed when American planes bombed the Japanese troop ship that was taking him and other prisoners of war to a Japanese prison.

Above, left: Private Robert Bellemare is shown in uniform. He served with the Eighteenth Air Depot Supply Squadron. *Courtesy of the Bennington Museum.*

Above, right: Captain Otto Bennett is shown in combat gear, rolling a cigarette. He served with Company I, 172nd Infantry, 43rd Division. *Courtesy of the Bennington Museum.*

Left: Edward Thomas Carroll in his navy uniform. *Courtesy of the Bennington Museum.*

We know that marine corporal John Schnurr was wounded on Saipan; that army infantryman Private First Class Robert W. Allen was wounded in Italy; that Private First Class Henry Ennis was wounded in the South Pacific; and that army first sergeant Daniel McGuire was wounded during the landing on D-Day.

We know that First Lieutenant Bernard Porter was reported missing in action in Luxembourg, the telegram arriving just as his wife was giving birth to a son at Putnam Hospital. He was captured during the Battle of the Bulge, escaped and was recaptured twice before a third escape allowed him to reach American lines. He later became a paratrooper and a career officer, seeing combat in Korea and retiring as a lieutenant colonel after twenty-six years of service. We know that marine private first class Rene Davignon was bayoneted three times—twice in the leg and once in the side—during hand-to-hand combat on Guam.

Captain Charles "Blackie" White of North Bennington was a West Point graduate who was killed when U.S. planes bombed a Japanese ship he was imprisoned on. *Courtesy of the* Bennington Banner.

We know that army private Leo Hill, twenty-six and married with two children, was killed in action in Belgium when he stepped on a land mine. We know that marine private first class Lawrence "Bud" Gates was killed on Iwo Jima. We know that Staff Sergeant Jeremy Graves of South Shaftsbury was killed in action in Germany; that air corps corporal Gilbert LaFlamme was killed in action in the Mediterranean; that Corporal Harry Harwood was killed on November 8, 1944, while serving with Patton's tanks. We know that Captain Leland Dunham was wounded in action while serving with Patton. He eventually because became executive officer of the First Battalion, Thirty-Fourth Infantry Regiment, Twenty-Fourth Infantry Division in Korea, where he was taken prisoner in South Korea after the defeat of the U.S. forces at Taejon on July 20, 1950. Along with much of his battalion, Dunham ended up on the so-called Tiger Death March, 120 miles over nine days, during which eighty-nine died, most of them shot and left for dead on the side of the road when they fell behind. Those shot included three women, two of them nuns. Dunham made it to the prisoner of war camp but died of beriberi on August 7, 1951, when he was just thirty-nine years old.

Many veterans went on to do very well. James Holden of North Bennington, a major in the Forty-Third Division in the South Pacific, became the chief judge of the Vermont Supreme Court. T. Gary Buckley of Bennington, who had been a glider pilot, became lieutenant governor. Margaret Lillie of Pownal became a state's attorney and probate judge, the first woman in Vermont to hold those jobs. William Kearns of Bennington became a major figure in state government, and Carleton Carpenter of Bennington became a star of the stage and screen. Norman Rockwell of Arlington didn't serve in the war, although he did serve briefly in World War I. But his famous "Four Freedoms" posters made millions of dollars when they were sold at war bond drives. And his "Rosie the Riveter"—whose name wasn't Rosie and who wasn't a riveter; she was a petite eighteen-year-old telephone operator in Arlington who he bulked up considerably—became a lasting symbol of the war effort at home.

In many ways, there was nothing special about Bennington's role in the war. A book like this could be written about thousands of other small towns all across the country. And yet, in the end, it *was* special. It was a special time that required a special commitment of discipline and sacrifice by ordinary people who were suddenly thrust into extraordinary situations. And while most of the people who served now are dead, all that they did should be remembered.

ABOUT THE AUTHOR

Anthony Marro was a reporter for the *Rutland* (Vermont) *Herald*, *Newsday*, *Newsweek* and the *New York Times*. From 1971 until 1981, he was based in Washington, D.C., where his coverage of the U.S. Department of Justice included extensive coverage of the Watergate scandal. He then spent six years as the managing editor and sixteen years as editor of *Newsday*, which was cited by *TIME* magazine and others as one of the ten best papers in the country.

Marro worked on reporting teams at *Newsday* that won Pulitzer Prize Gold Medals for public service reporting in 1970 and 1974. The paper won twelve more Pulitzer Prize Gold Medals during his time as an editor. He also is a co-author of *Beyond the Hiss Case: The FBI, Congress and the Cold War* and *Philip Hoff: How Red Turned Blue in the Green Mountain State*.

He and his wife, Jacqueline, now split their time evenly between Bennington, Vermont, and North Scituate, Rhode Island, where they tend large gardens and keep bees and where he often writes about Vermont people, places and history.